NEW VENTURE ANALYSIS

RESEARCH, PLANNING AND FINANCE

NEW VENTURE ANALYSIS

RESEARCH, PLANNING AND FINANCE

Dennis R. Costello

DOW JONES-IRWIN
Homewood, Illinois 60430

© DOW JONES-IRWIN, 1985

This publication is designed to provide accurate and
authoritative information in regard to the subject matter
covered. It is sold with the understanding that the
publisher is not engaged in rendering legal, accounting, or
other professional service. If legal advice or other expert
assistance is required, the services of a competent
professional person should be sought.

*From a Declaration of Principles jointly adopted by a Committee
of the American Bar Association and a Committee of Publishers.*

ISBN 0-87094-505-X

Library of Congress Catalog Card No. 84-73197

Printed in the United States of America

1 2 3 4 5 6 7 8 9 0 K 2 1 0 9 8 7 6 5

To Kathryn, Matthew and Lauren

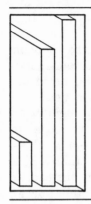

Foreword

Intrapreneuring is a word that has yet to make its way into our dictionaries, but the words *risk* and *venture* are ones we know well. If this volume succeeds in taking some of the risk out of corporate venturing, it will have served business and society very well indeed.

Our ability to innovate and manage change is one that we can and must build upon if the United States is to continue as the economic engine of the free world and if its strengths are to continue buoying the economies of other nations.

Most organizations begin with a small team of people and, if their venture is successful, the organization begins to grow. Things change. With growth comes a tendency to wall off new ideas into separate compartments surrounded by specialists. Boundaries emerge and people can become fenced in like sheep in a pasture.

To perpetuate the original vitality of the organization becomes a challenge, one that is faced by many large firms today. An essential step in maintaining or renewing vitality in an organization is to provide a system for the care and feeding of innovators and their new ventures. It seems clear to me that, without a commitment from the top, innovation will be defeated again and again by the policies, procedures, and rituals of almost any large organization.

It is tempting to believe that the planner or manager and the innovator are natural adversaries. Tempting, but not necessarily true. Managers want order and accountability; innovators thrive on freedom and creativity. Yet there is much that management can do to create and foster a climate that stimulates innovation. It is management's job to assess opportunities, compare alternative strategies, allocate resources wisely, and lay down the challenge. It is management that stimulates good cross-communication. It is management that rewards achievement, and at the same time accepts honest mistakes and failures without harsh penalities. Often it takes faith and patience and patient money. To borrow a line from *Finian's Rainbow,*we sometimes have to "follow the fellow who follows a dream."

This does not mean that innovation or venturing need be a random process. When innovation or venturing work, they work because someone has identified a real need and has found a way to bring new ideas or new technologies to bear on that need. This link between needs and innovation suggests that a successful venture strategy ought to be based on conditions within an industry, rather than on hopes or dreams alone. Unless one has a base of information about markets, customers, and competitors, the plan becomes little more than a hope or a guess as to what will happen. We prefer a plan that is, instead, an informed decision about what we want to happen, one that tells how we will go about making it happen.

My entire business career has been with a company long known for its pervasive internal venturing programs. At 3M, we like to see 25 percent of each year's sales generated from products or services that were new in the previous five years. If any of our products are to become obsolete, we prefer to be the ones who render them obsolete.

Each of our more than 40 division managers is charged with developing new business ventures and spinning them off. This policy of dividing for growth is based in part on a discovery we made years ago. When an operating unit reaches a certain size, it has a tendency to spend its time on established products or markets. It then has less time to spend on new ventures. We find that when we break out a new business and give people an opportunity to identify with it, almost inevitably the new unit begins to grow at a faster rate. New ventures are, thus, a part of our own renewal process in every division.

Have we always succeeded? No—but we have managed to survive and grow. Have we done it all by the book? Not at all; there has been no book. Now there is.

Lewis W. Lehr
Chairman of the Board and
Chief Executive Officer
3M

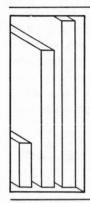

Preface

This book is about ideas—ideas on how to do a better job dealing with new ventures within your company. It is intended to give practicing business managers, analysts, and business students ideas about how to select the most promising research and development projects; ideas about how to better understand the markets, competitors, costs, and uncertainties facing your new ventures; ideas about how to finance your new ventures; and even ideas on how to generate new venture ideas.

I have tried to fill this book with ideas without becoming too idealistic. The book is intended to be a book of change. We have all been reading about "corporate cultures." The most debilitating aspect of our increased awareness of corporate cultures is that we are almost powerless to change them. By definition, your company's culture represents its most deep-seated values, beliefs, and philosophies. Changing that culture is equivalent to changing your own personality. I do not believe that most of us will ever be in a position to change our company's culture, even if we are the chief executive officer. Similar to the way we view the prospect of changing our own personality, few of us, I think, believe that changing our corporation's culture would bring about an improvement.

The changes that are possible within your company are those which incrementally improve the quality of decisions made concerning key aspects of the business. New ventures are among the most important of these changes. I have aimed this book at the practical issues that surround new ventures within an existing firm. More thoughtful new venture decisions, based on better understanding, can produce tangible benefits for you, your company, and the entire economy.

The ideas and techniques I will present are not all my original thoughts. Approaches have been gathered from numerous fields such as strategic planning, market research, operations research, and finance and have then been applied to new venture settings. I have relied on the work of other business authors to augment my experience with new ventures. The combination of our experiences and approaches is intended to give you a starting point to better analyze new ventures at your company.

I wish you the creativity needed to apply these techniques and the courage to introduce changes in the way your company makes new venture decisions.

Dennis Costello

Contents

1

Introduction

The ability of industrialized nations to develop new technologies and translate them into useful products will be crucial to world economic growth in the 1980s and 1990s. Technological advances are already playing an increasingly important role in the world economy. Technology is producing higher quality goods with more capabilities and often at a lower cost. Those firms and nations that can remain at the forefront of technology will assure themselves a preeminent role in world economic growth. Those without the resources or capability to keep pace with technological advances will find it more and more difficult to maintain their economic status. The United States, Canada, Japan, and most of the nations of Western Europe have already recognized the role of technology and have taken action to improve their technological base. Within the United States, competition for technology-based economic growth is evident at the regional, state, and even local levels.

National, state, and local governments can try to stimulate technology-based economic growth, but the private sector is at the front lines of this emerging form of world economic competition. The ability of a corporation to translate new technology into salable goods and services will largely determine its future national and international economic success.

Much has been written recently about start-up companies and the role of entrepreneurs in technological advancement—a role that cannot be denied. What is often overlooked, however, is the larger role of

1

established medium- to large-sized firms. Many of the most economically successful technological innovations have been introduced by established companies. IBM's personal computer (PC) is one of the best recent examples. The IBM PC may not have represented the edge of technological innovation when it was introduced, but IBM's ability to rapidly introduce technology into the consumer sector cannot be disputed. New ventures into computer time sharing and on-line data base services by aerospace companies such as Boeing, Lockheed, McDonnell Douglas, and TRW have also yielded large returns. A major new venture into satellite-based business communication services is underway as a joint venture between IBM and Aetna Life and Casualty. AT&T's new venture into office information services and personal computers also illustrates the role of established firms in new ventures.

Introducing new products or services is not a simple task for an existing company. If a new product is significantly different from a company's existing business, the problem is many times more difficult: we call the latter situation a new venture. In the pages that follow, we will investigate the analytical tools that can help existing companies make the difficult decisions surrounding their internal new ventures. We will begin with corporate research and development projects. Our discussion will parallel the evolution of the new venture from a research project to an ongoing, successful product line. We will discuss how new markets, costs, competitors, and uncertainty can be evaluated in a new venture setting. Most importantly, we will explain how these analyses of individual aspects of a new venture can be combined into a consistent framework for evaluation. Various ways to review your firm's entire portfolio of new ventures will be explored. Finally, the delicate issue of seeking external sources of finance for internal new ventures will be addressed.

Setting

Established companies do not launch new ventures based on perceived needs to keep their domicile nation at the forefront of technology. Even arguments that the company should maintain a technological leadership position are often not strong enough justification for multi-million dollar investments in a new venture. The need for new ventures most commonly arises out of the firm's more general strategic planning process. Most of a firm's planning activities revolve around its current portfolio of businesses or industries. Actions to maintain, expand, or change the position of that portfolio relative to the competitive market environment are the tangible results of the planning process. Many firms will also periodically review their business portfolio from a longer term perspective to determine if the firm's direction is meeting basic corporate goals. Probably an equal number of firms change their long-term goals if the industries in which they are successful fall outside their original objectives.

In either case, forecasts of life cycles of the products that comprise the firm's portfolio may show that a gap will develop between the firm's financial goals and the expected performance of its existing businesses. That gap is commonly labeled a "planning gap" or a "sales gap." Figure 1–1 illustrates the gap. When senior management identifies a planning gap, they are often motivated to take action. The actions suggested may include launching one or more new ventures.

The term *new ventures* probably has as many definitions as there are articles written about the subject. For our purposes, we will define a new venture as a segregated activity within a firm that is devoted to

FIGURE 1–1
Planning or Sales Gap

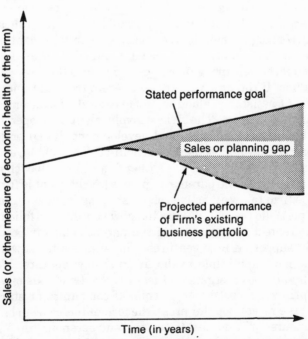

Source: Reprinted by permission of the publisher from "New Venture Planning: The Role of Technological Forecasting," by Wade Blackman, *Technological Forecasting and Social Change* **5**, pp. 25–49, copyright 1973 by Elsevier Science Publishing Co., Inc.

the exploitation of a novel business situation. The activity is accounted for separately from the firm's regular operations and has a distinct group of technical and managerial staff assigned to it. New ventures then deal with products that are significantly different from the firm's current products. The firm's management and its existing customers do not consider these products to be extensions of or minor changes to existing lines. New ventures can yield products that have not yet been introduced by competitors. Recently, they have often had a strong technological base. They usually serve markets not traditionally served by the company. If they are introduced into existing markets, they must be sufficiently distinct from current products for customers to recognize a marked difference in the character of their purchases.

As we begin to explore the definition of new ventures in more detail, it becomes obvious that a firm is faced with a continuum of options, beginning with existing products and progressing through new products to new ventures. It is not possible and probably not even useful to find precise definitions that can clearly separate the sections of this continuum. Thus, the definition we have outlined here is intended to give a general impression of what is covered by the term *new ventures*.

Even within the general field of new ventures, you can find an array of activities. Edward Roberts (1980) has arranged these forms of activity according to their degree of corporate involvement (see Figure 1–2). The figure shows that the least amount of corporate involvement is required if the venturing firm merely provides the new venture with capital funds. If the new venture gets direct technical, marketing, or management assistance along with the capital, the parent company's involvement increases. The firm's involvement is deeper if the new venture begins as a research and development (R&D) project and is later separated through some type of spin-off. The next level of involvement is active joint ventures with other firms in which each must meet certain obligations. The parent company's involvement is further deepened if the firm takes an active role in shaping its new ventures into a cohesive portfolio (we will discuss the new venture portfolio in Chapter 10). The greatest involvement of the parent company occurs within internally supported new ventures. The analysis framework we will develop is most applicable to the internal new venture. We will not specifically address mergers and less involved methods of venturing.

Our primary focus is not on spin-off companies or start-up companies. In the recent popular press, the former has come to be known as "intrapreneurship" and the latter as "entrepreneurship." An *intra*-preneur creates his or her new products within an established company, while an *entre*preneur creates a new company to pursue his or her interests. The same types of issues have to be faced in either case.

FIGURE 1–2
Roberts's Schematic of Alternative New Venture Strategies

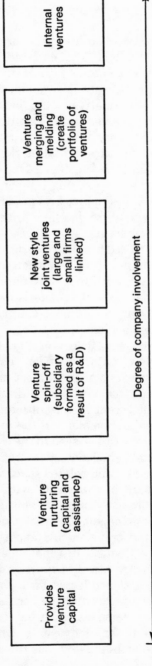

| Provides venture capital | Venture nurturing (capital and assistance) | Venture spin-off (subsidiary formed as a result of R&D) | New style joint ventures (large and small firms linked) | Venture merging and melding (create portfolio of ventures) | Internal ventures |

Degree of company involvement

Less ————————————————————→ More

Source: Reprinted by permission of the *Harvard Business Review*. An exhibit from "New Ventures for Corporate Growth," by Edward Roberts (July/August 1980). Copyright © 1980 by the President and Fellows of Harvard College; all rights reserved.

We believe that the techniques and guidelines discussed here have strong applicability to start-up companies. However, the special problems involved in starting a new company will not be separately addressed.

One major difference between intrapreneurs and entrepreneurs is the number of objective appraisals that each must face before a product reaches consumers. The entrepreneur finds an idea to which she is personally committed and pursues it. The mechanism for sorting out the value of his or her idea relative to the ideas of others is the free enterprise system. External and sometimes bitterly objective markets determine whether the idea has value. The first market faced by the entrepreneur is often the venture capital market. The pursuit of venture capital funds sorts ideas: It involves a type of market that has no parallel mechanism within an existing company. The analysis techniques to be presented are designed to give guidance to senior management as they make new venture decisions without the objectivity of external venture capital markets.

The final market test faced by a new venture is the same no matter how the venture is organized. It occurs when potential consumers of the product decide whether or not to make a purchase. The value of the analytical techniques that we will explore is measured by how effectively corporate resources are used during the months and years before that ultimate market test begins.

In the context of an ongoing firm, a new venture is of considerable strategic importance. New venture decisions do not arise very often. However, such decisions can be of the utmost importance to the company's future performance—or even its continuing existence. Even a casual observation of the recent history of many firms demonstrates that there is a need for improvement in the quality of new venture decisions. A typical example can be seen in the Grumman Corporation. Grumman is a well-established aerospace company specializing in naval aircraft. Their aircraft and related space vehicle contracts gave them a significant amount of experience with high technology and with the integration of large, complex systems. Based on their annual reports, it appears that a management decision was made to undertake new ventures that would transfer this expertise to new markets. Grumman pursued new products in renewable energy and in mass transit. Their flexible bus venture (acquired through an acquisition from Rohr Industries) has shown losses since its inception. Structural defects were found in the buses and the company sustained further losses. The ventures—in particular, the buses—caused Grumman's profits to remain unstable for many years. Only recently, as those ventures have been sold or liquidated, has the strong performance of

Grumman's original military airplane business been again reflected in the company's corporate profits.

Hundreds of other unsuccessful new ventures have been launched within existing companies. Many have severely hampered the financial performance of the firm's original product portfolio and even more have merely been a drain on corporate resources without yielding any long-term benefits.

Many of the analytical tools developed by management scientists, market researchers, and strategic planners can be used to improve the quality of new venture decisions. Some examples of the application of these tools to new ventures can be found in the business literature (see, for example, Beattie, 1969; Blackman, 1973; Costello, 1978; and Urban & Hauser, 1980). Predictably, each study approaches the problem using different tools and from a slightly different perspective. These studies, however, are the exception rather than the rule in the new venture arena. More commonly, new venture commitments are made with inadequate or nonexistent analyses. We will try to help reverse that condition in the chapters that follow. It is not necessary to invent new analytic techniques when dealing with new ventures, for there is a more than adequate tool kit available from other fields of business research. What *is* required is the creative adaptation of those tools to the unique characteristics of new ventures. Creative modification of existing techniques will be a recurring theme in the following chapters.

What Is the Real Problem?

The words and phrases that come to mind when successful new ventures are reviewed are: *innovation, insight, risk taking, boldness,* and *unconventional thinking.* These are certainly key attributes of the new venture process. However, perhaps one of the most important and most often overlooked attribute is clear thinking. Clear thinking in the new venture arena needs to begin with a succinct statement of what a company is trying to accomplish and how. In consonance with this need, let us review the major problems that we will address in the chapters ahead.

First, we have to determine what types of analytic techniques are available that can address new venture decisions. Second, we have to determine how these techniques can be applied to improve new venture decisions. In this regard, the most important decisions are those dealing with the commitment of scarce corporate resources such as capital, key personnel, and management's time.

To address these major problems, a set of more limited questions must be answered. These include: (1) What analytical tools have already been used to support new venture decisions? (2) What other tools or techniques have the potential to be applied? and (3) Can a framework or set of guidelines be developed to help analysts and managers use the available tools in a more consistent and effective manner?

The Problem in Context

The problems outlined above would be a significant challenge if the new venture decision of interest was confined to a single point in time, presumably just before significant capital funds were committed. However, the decision to begin a new venture in a medium- or large-sized corporation is not made at a single point in time. Rather, the decision is a process that may continue over months or even years and may involve many levels of management. During this process, there are numerous key points at which crucial "Go or No Go" decisions have to be made.

Almost by definition, new ventures are alien to the cultures of most corporations and often face many more decision hurdles than decisions involving the company's more traditional products. Our experience has shown that whenever the corporation is confronted with external stress, new venture decisions are reevaluated. Sales declines, losses of market share to competitors, technological challenges, direct cost growth, overhead cost growth, or similar events cause companies to review their research and development and new product budgets. Existing product areas, when threatened by budget cuts, will naturally point to the new venture portfolio as an area for cost savings. New ventures are therefore faced with many more "No Go" decision hurdles than the rest of the product line. They probably also face more of these hurdles than smaller, start-up companies funded by external venture capital sources. Most managers realize the obvious pitfall of sacrificing long-term viability for short-term financial gain. Many firms have instituted highly successful procedures to protect R&D and new ventures from these types of financial fluctuations. In other firms, the procedures tend to crumble under the pressure of quarterly profit goals.

Of all the decision points that face a new venture, perhaps the most important occurs after the product has been developed and market tested, and the decision of whether to build a full-scale commercial production facility or to shelve the idea must be made. This is a crucial point in the new venture process because (1) a single decision will be made that involves large sums of capital for production, (2) this commitment of resources is largely irrevocable, and (3) the maximum amount of empirical data is available to the decision maker short of the results from full-scale introduction. At this point, many companies may conduct a detailed evaluation, termed a *venture analysis*. The same situation is faced if the firm is considering an acquisition rather than an internally generated new venture.

The other key decision points in the new venture process are also important. The first of these is often the decision to fund a research and development (R&D) project. In many companies, R&D is the first stage in the development of a new venture. R&D projects may be selected to fill consumer needs that have been identified by previous market research. They may also be selected based on the interest of the firm's research or managerial staff. In either case, the decision is constrained due to scarce resources. Keeping in mind budget limitations, the manager must select a portfolio of R&D projects that will maximize expected economic value to the firm. (We will revisit the concept of economic value creation in Chapter 2.)

Another key decision point occurs when a new product is about to enter the demonstration or prototype phase. The amount of resources necessary to design and build a prototype will vary tremendously depending on the technology or process under consideration and the capabilities of the firm. If significant funds are required, this decision becomes one more step that is crucial to the new venture's existence. Other decisions that may be significant include (1) funds allocated for initial market studies, (2) funds and time allocated for idea generation, and (3) budget allocations for test marketing.

The difficult and sequential nature of the new venture decision process adds considerable complexity to the issue of applying analytic techniques to support those decisions. Figure 1–3, a generalized flow chart of the new venture decision process, divides the process into five separable steps. Step 1 is the identification of a planning gap. As we mentioned earlier, this identification is a direct result of the firm's strategic planning process or the convictions of senior management. Step 2 is probably the most creative part of the venture process. Here, ideas are generated which are later separated and selected. The emphasis at this stage is on expansive thinking. Steps 3 and 4 contain decision points that require selecting among competing ideas. In step 3, ideas are advanced through either R&D projects or product development projects. Corporate resources must be committed to fund these projects. However, the major resource requirements occur when production facilities are constructed (step 4). Decisions at this step limit the number of new ventures more severely than decisions in step 3. The final step of the process is the decision to launch the product, service, or technology and to manage the venture as an element of the

FIGURE 1-3
Generalized Flow of the New Venture Process within an Existing Company

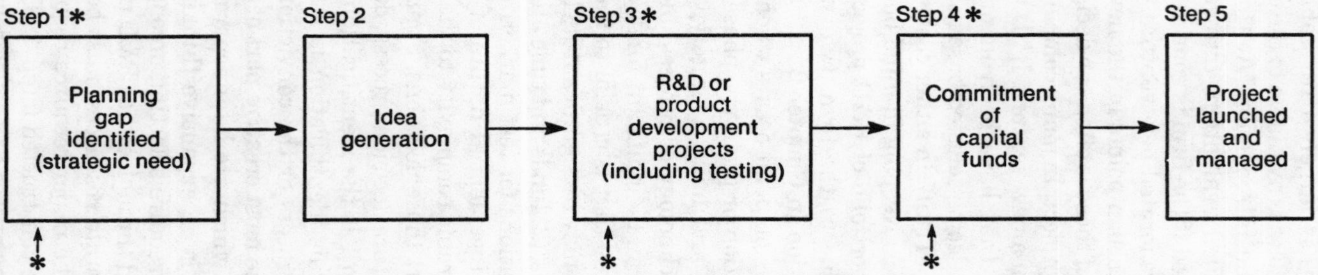

Step 1*	Step 2	Step 3*	Step 4*	Step 5
Planning gap identified (strategic need)	Idea generation	R&D or product development projects (including testing)	Commitment of capital funds	Project launched and managed

* Analysis needed at these points.

business portfolio. When the project becomes part of the current business portfolio, we no longer call it a new venture.

These five simplified steps provide a convenient mechanism for segregating the new venture process. We have used them to organize the chapters that follow and to divide the new venture decision process into its components. First, analytical techniques applicable to each step will be examined separately. Then, we will discuss how to integrate those techniques into a cogent analysis that will yield useful results.

Objective and Scope

Our primary objective is to develop a consistent framework for analyzing new venture decisions. That framework will be of practical use to decision makers because it will effectively incorporate a large number of analytical techniques, which could improve the quality of the decisions that are made. The framework will provide an organized and consistent perspective for approaching the five steps described above. It will also provide some guidelines for determining which analytical tools are potentially useful in each step of the decision process.

We will not develop any completely new techniques for use in new venture issues. Our intent is not to push back the frontiers of management science. Rather, we will examine, modify, and integrate existing tools that have been developed in fields such as strategic business planning, market research, and competitor assessment. Uncertainty is the overriding feature of any new venture. The evaluation of uncertainty and its comparisons with alternative new ventures will be a critical element in our discussions.

In summary, our analytic framework will be designed to meet the following eight specific criteria:

1. It should be objective and not easily biased by personnel involved in developing or managing the new venture.
2. It should be internally consistent in its comparison of new ventures and across the five steps of the venture process (as shown in Figure 1-3).
3. It should allow new information to be incorporated into the analysis as it becomes available.
4. It should be a vehicle for communication among all groups involved in the new venture.
5. It should allow competing new venture ideas to be easily compared.

6. It should adequately reflect the differences in uncertainty surrounding competing new ventures.
7. It should be flexible enough to be useful in a variety of new venture situations.
8. It should remain as simple as possible and be understandable to decision makers.

2

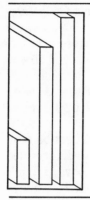

An Analytical Framework for New Venture Decisions

The Creation of Economic Value

Whether you are the manager or the analyst, the practical aspects of a new venture analysis quickly becomes engrossing. The constant threat to everyone involved is the loss of a broad perspective on the basic issues. We have found that a brief time spent examining new ventures from a broader perspective is important to avoiding this pitfall.

In its simplest terms, a new venture must help a corporation achieve its basic goals. Although economists argue about those goals, we will settle for one of the more prominent conventional definitions: The basic goal of any firm in a competitive market environment is to create economic value for its owners. Many vastly different types of strategies may be pursued by firms at different times and under different circumstances to achieve this goal. Each of these strategies, however, is aimed at the creation and sustenance of economic value. The goal of every new venture then must be to create economic value for the firm's owners.

It is important to have a good grasp of the meaning of the term *economic value*. A good or service has economic value if individuals are willing to give up scarce resources to obtain it. In the context of a corporation, an asset has economic value if it yields returns to the firm in excess of its costs. All firms compete to create economic value. The marketplace is the independent and collective judge of their relative success; it determines the economic value of the assets held by a firm.

We can further define the concept of economic value by using the concept of present values. The economic value of an asset (or an entire company), as reflected by the market, is the stream of net income or net returns generated by that asset over its useful life. Of course, the value of that income partly depends on when it is generated. To take these differences of timing into account, we use the present value concept. Future income is discounted to its equivalent present value. Thus, the present value of any sum of money to be received in the future is the amount of money that would yield that sum, including interest, if placed in an interest bearing account today. (A more extensive discussion of the present value concept can be found in Weston and Brigham, 1981.)

Any firm's dilemma in creating economic values can best be seen as a problem of optimizing an objective (reaching a predetermined goal) that is subject to a series of constraints. As stated above, a firm's basic objective or goal is to maximize its economic value. To achieve this goal, the firm has control of a limited number of factors such as which assets to hold and when to divest assets, as well as a limited set of actions to prevent competitors from diluting the economic value of those assets. In addition, the firm has some short-term control over how much information is available to its owners and to the market. The amount of available information will influence how the market values the company. Constraints facing the firm include limited resources, technological limitations, and limited knowledge of consumers, competitors, and government.

New ventures should be viewed as one way for a firm to maximize the creation of economic value. Alternatively, new ventures can represent an effort to *re*create a large amount of economic value after a poor performance period. In either case, the analyses and decisions that are made must capture the essence of the new venture's objective of economic value creation. Any new venture analysis must ultimately measure (1) the amount of economic value that the new venture could potentially create, (2) the relative uncertainty of achieving that result, (3) the degree to which your firm can expect to prevent competitors from diluting that value, and (4) the degree to which the owners of the parent company and the users of the new venture's product(s) will recognize your venture's value.

We cannot overstress the importance of keeping the basic concept of economic value in mind throughout the new venture analysis process. There are numerous examples of corporate decisions that ignore this concept. One of the best documented set of examples is the wave of business acquisitions and mergers that occurred in the United States during the 1960s and 1970s. Although acquisitions are a special type of new venture which we do not intend to spend much time on, they represent corporate decisions that are similar in nature to new venture decisions.

The size of the corporate acquisitions wave mentioned above is illustrated in Figure 2-1. The figure shows the number of manufacturing and mining firms acquired between 1895 and 1978 (other industries could also be used as examples). Although mergers and acquisitions seem to follow a cyclical pattern, the largest increase occurred after 1965. The majority of the latter acquisitions were made by companies in unrelated businesses. The economic value created by the acquiring firms has to be seriously questioned and many studies have done that. Those studies have concluded that the performance of conglomerates indicates that "unrelated diversification is not a panacea for lagging corporate performance" (Salter & Weinhold, 1979, p. 27). The case against acquisition to create economic value has been

FIGURE 2-1
Number of Manufacturing and Mining Firms Acquired, 1895–1978

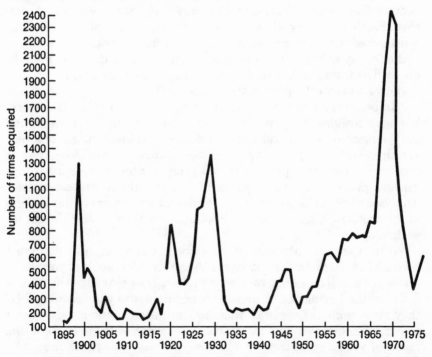

taken even further. For example, Mason and Goudzwaard (1976) conclude that "our results indicate that randomly selected portfolios offered superior earnings performance and shareholder returns than did the conglomerates in our sample" (p. 48). Although less evidence is available, many internally generated new ventures also fail to create economic value.

The New Venture Decision Analysis Framework

The transition from thinking about creating economic value to completing a new venture analysis is difficult and time consuming. To do the job efficiently, some type of conceptual framework is needed.

A wide variety of new venture analysis frameworks has appeared in the economic and business literature. These frameworks have many elements in common but usually differ in emphasis. We have synthesized and modified them to produce a comprehensive approach.

In the pages that follow, we will first review our synthesized new venture framework. Next, we will review other frameworks and compare them with our synthesized approach. Figure 2–2 summarizes our synthesized new venture decision analysis framework. Each element of the framework describes one type of analysis or action that must be taken. The framework is designed to allow ideas to cycle through it at various stages in the new venture process.

To begin the analysis, a new venture idea enters the framework. We have designed the framework to be used both in the research and development selection and in the capital expenditure stages of a new venture. That is, ideas may enter the framework as R&D ideas or product development proposals, and then reenter as a detailed new venture proposal before major capital expenditures are committed. Analyses at both stages should be consistent and cover similar aspects of the problem, although the level of detail will be quite different for each stage.

After the idea enters the framework, the first analysis you must conduct is a check for consistency with the strategic goals of your firm. These goals will certainly vary across firms. They may take the form of defining the businesses or industries of interest to your company. Or they may represent specific orders or limitations announced by your senior management. The most probable source of these goals is the result of your firm's strategic planning process. This check may take only a few minutes or it may require review by corporate executives and planning committees. It is the simplest yet one of the most important steps in the venture analysis framework.

FIGURE 2–2
The New Venture Analysis Framework

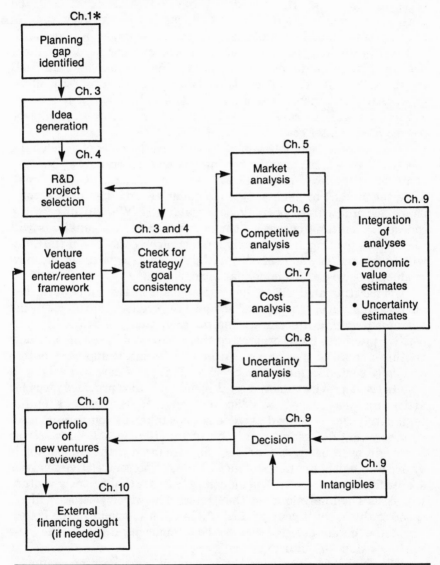

* Indicates chapter where techniques are presented.

The core of the new venture analysis framework is the four types of analyses shown in the middle of Figure 2–2 (that is, market, competition, cost, and uncertainty analysis). The market analysis must determine the need for the product, the effective demand, and the consumer's reaction to the product at various prices. A variety of market research and technological diffusion techniques are available to assist in this task (see Chapter 5). A brief assessment of consumer need may be adequate to evaluate ideas being considered for an R&D project. When the new venture is ready for production investments, a great deal of empirically based market information will be necessary. Techniques such as consumer surveys and test marketing may be needed at this later stage.

The second type of key analysis examines the costs of developing, producing, distributing, and servicing products generated by your new venture. At the R&D project selection stage, the analysis may break down the product by general types of materials and then predict costs using learning curves of analogous materials. (We will discuss the concept of learning curves in Chapter 7.) Later, cost analyses will require engineering drawings and production process flowcharts. Costs will be broken down in much more detailed categories as the new product gets closer to commercial introduction.

Competitive analysis is the next element of the framework. Explicit evaluation of competitors' actions is a recent development in the business planning literature. Traditionally, analyses deal with competitive pressures by incorporating them into predictions of your new venture's share of the market. Although the latter approach is theoretically correct, a more explicit investigation of how and why such results occur provides many useful insights. It also provides ideas for actions that may prevent or reduce the impact of a competitor's retaliation. Retaliation is defined as those actions taken by competitors after your new venture product is introduced into the market. Such actions can begin even before the product is introduced if the competitor is aware of the pending new product offering. The competitive analysis should first try to identify the industry structure that the new venture will face. The analysis must then forecast how competitors will respond to the entry of your product. As in other elements of the framework, the detail pursued has to be commensurate with the new venture's stage of maturity.

The fourth analytic element is explicit consideration of uncertainty. The relative uncertainty of a new venture is as important as its expected net cash flow. The new venture decision should not necessarily attempt to minimize risk; however, decision makers should expect that higher risk ventures will offer higher expected returns.

Measurement of uncertainty is not a highly developed field in either management science or marketing research. Simple approaches to measuring relative uncertainty may be used when R&D projects are being selected, and more rigorous approaches may be used before larger capital investment decisions are made.

The four analyses shown in the middle of Figure 2-2, (market, competition, cost, and uncertainty) have to be combined to complete an evaluation of the new venture. Thus, the next element of the framework integrates these four analyses and considers their interactions. When dealing with R&D project ideas, the integration may be quite simple. Its objective is to determine the net expected economic value of the idea and to assign some measure of relative uncertainty. These summary measures should be used to compare alternative ideas and to reach R&D funding decisions. At the later stage of the new venture process, a more detailed integration has to be conducted. It is at the later stage that most new venture analysts develop models. (We will be reviewing the key elements of those models in Chapter 9.) Sensitivity analyses are conducted on the model and probabilistic modeling can be introduced to more fully evaluate the uncertainty of the venture. Decisions are made following the integration phase.

The last elements in the framework are a review of all the firm's new ventures from a portfolio perspective and sometimes the obtaining of external financing. In a larger company, there should be numerous new ventures underway at the same time. We have found it most helpful to evaluate the strategic implications of this series of independent new venture decisions. Tools are available that can help to determine the diversification or concentration of risk inherent in your firm's new venture portfolio. Recent advances in strategic planning are the source of these tools.

Review of Alternative Frameworks

At this point, it is useful to review some of the new venture analysis frameworks that have been presented in the literature and to compare them to our framework. We have saved all comparisons of specific analytical techniques used in each framework for later chapters and concentrated only on the overall frameworks here.

Blackman's Framework

Wade Blackman (1973) created a system for planning new ventures which integrates technological forecasting, decision analysis, and system dynamics. Blackman prescribes a two-step screening process. The first step is designed to be done quickly and at low cost. It requires the following seven sequential actions:

1. Define needs.
2. Define products that fit.
3. Estimate manufacturing cost.
4. Decide if the product can be made more cheaply than one made by competitors.
5. Estimate the value to the consumer relative to its selling price.
6. Estimate market characteristics and sales.
7. Check sales estimates with business requirements.

The actions of Blackman's first-step screening process are similar to those in ours (Figure 2-2) except (1) the order of the analyses is different, and (2) Blackman does not explicitly evaluate uncertainty. The order in which the analyses are conducted is not particularly crucial if the analyses are all completed before decisions are made. The lack of treatment of uncertainty is a more serious problem.

The second step in Blackman's screening process is a more detailed venture analysis in which the construction of a computer-based model and the treatment of uncertainty are both integral parts. Figure 2-3 summarizes the Blackman model.

The inputs to Blackmans second-step framework are shown on the left side of the figure. Many of them deal with the costs of launching a new venture, but some require understanding the market that your new venture will enter. There is obviously a great deal of work required to generate these inputs. We will discuss our approach to these problems later. The middle of the figure lists various models that comprise Blackman's overall new venture analysis framework, and can be viewed as subroutines of a larger integrating model that produces projections of sales, cash flows, and risks. The outputs are internally consistent and of obvious interest to decision makers.

Blackman's model emphasizes costs, market share, and uncertainty. This part of Blackman's approach is similar to ours in most respects. There are only two significant differences. First, competitive analysis is handled only through estimates of market share and market substitutions. Second, Blackman's treatment of uncertainty is extensive but does not analyze risk versus return trade-offs to derive a new ventures portfolio. Rank ordering of investment opportunities based on cash flows is conducted to derive Blackman's selections.

Rank ordering of investments raises an important overriding issue in the analysis of new ventures. The extensive analysis of risk is only of value if the results are adequately appreciated by the decision makers. If the richness of the uncertainty analysis is lost in a simple

FIGURE 2–3
Blackman's Venture Analysis Model Flowchart

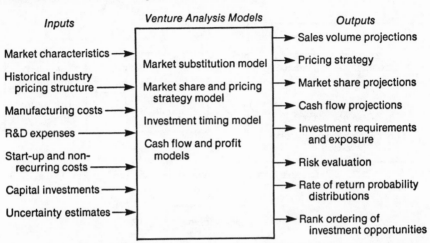

Source: Reprinted by permission of the publisher from "New Venture Planning: The Role of Technological Forecasting," by Wade Blackman, *Technological Forecasting and Social Change* 5, pp. 25–49. Copyright 1973 by Elsevier Science Publishing Co., Inc.

rank ordering of the results, it is of no value. A simplified presentation of your results is always an appropriate goal. However, if that simplicity masks key success drivers, you are doing a disservice to your management. We will discuss results presentation in more detail in a later chapter.

Urban and Urban/Hauser Frameworks

Glen Urban's approach to new venture evaluation (Urban, 1968) is a one-step, detailed analysis that is intended to be conducted prior to a major capital expenditure. As shown in the top section of Figure 2–4, the major parts of the analysis are demand and cost estimation procedures: these are integrated by the model. The model maximizes profit by varying factors that are under the firm's control. Uncertainty and risk-return trade-offs are treated explicitly in Urban's framework. The demand estimation element in Urban's model includes an assessment of the competition.

Some of the drawbacks of Urban's original approach are explained by Lipstein (1968). Lipstein concludes that: (1) new venture decisions are sequential refinements, but Urban presents a framework oriented around a single decision; (2) the research funds allocation procedure is

FIGURE 2–4
Urban's New Product Analysis Model and Urban/Hauser's New Product Development Process

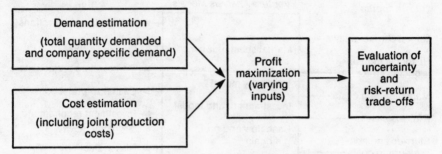

Urban's New Product Analysis Model, 1968

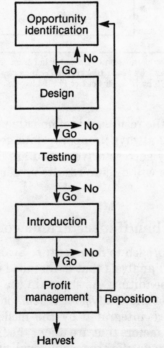

Urban and Hauser's New Product Development Process, 1980

Source: Top figure reprinted by permission of Glen L. Urban, "A New Product Analysis and Decision Model," *Management Science* 14, no. 8 (April 1968), Copyright 1968, The Institute of Management Sciences.

Bottom figure, Glen L. Urban and John R. Hauser, *Design and Marketing of New Products,* © 1980, p. 33. Reprinted by permission of Prentice-Hall, Inc., Englewood Cliffs, N.J.

the first step in the venture process, but Urban ignores that step. In addition, the combining of market and competitive analysis makes the analysis of each more difficult.

Urban's original model is one of the few we reviewed that maximizes profit rather than just projecting a single economic outcome for the new venture. By maximizing profit in the model, the analysis serves the function of a decision maker. Most new venture frameworks merely predict the results of the decision maker's action (that is, they simulate a set of results based on one set of inputs). Thus, one can view models that maximize or optimize a predetermined objective as attempts to replace decision makers rather than support them. However, even simulations can be manipulated to usurp rather than support decision makers' prerogatives. We do not believe, therefore, that the choice between simulation and maximization models should be based on these arguments. The predominance of simulation modeling in new ventures appears to be due primarily to the complexity of the problems being addressed. However, a secondary reason for their use should be sensitivity to the needs and requests of your senior management.

The original framework developed by Urban was significantly expanded in scope and coverage in a recent book by Urban and Hauser (1980). The latter framework (shown at the bottom of Figure 2–4) addresses the introduction of new products. Most new product introductions are not new ventures; however, new ventures must be considered a special type of new product introduction.

Urban and Hauser's refined framework begins with opportunity identification and ends with profit management. It emphasizes design and testing throughout the development process and is substantially more comprehensive that Urban's earlier framework. The constant checking of the new product development with market realities is vital and should be a crucial ingredient in any new venture.

Hax and Wiig Framework

The Hax and Wiig framework (1976) was developed to analyze any major capital investment—not only new ventures. Therefore, the approach ignores R&D project selection and other preliminary screening stages. The authors analyzed a capital decision of an unnamed mining company that was considering an expansion in its supply capacity. Their approach, summarized in Figure 2–5, differs in two ways from the other frameworks reviewed. First, it does not assume that a simple, onetime Go or No Go decision has to be made. Rather, it allows a variety of actions to be combined to maximize benefits to the company

FIGURE 2–5
Haig and Wiig Capital Decision Analysis Framework

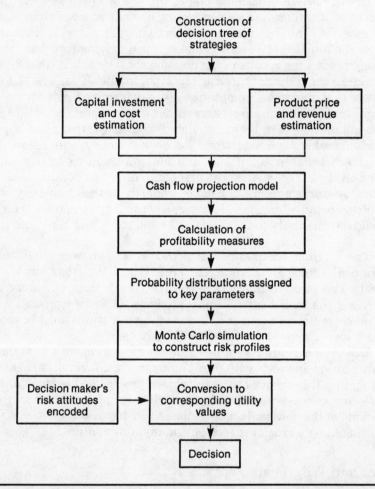

(26 separate strategies are identified). Second, the risk preferences of the decision makers are explicitly incorporated into the analysis. Analyses of the market and competitive responses are not considered the major source of uncertainty, and are not treated in detail. Cost estimates are handled in a manner similar to that of the other frameworks. Although one competing capital project is compared to the

capital decision, the decision is not viewed as an element of a corporate investment portfolio.

Costello et al.'s Framework

It is also appropriate to compare our current framework with some of our own earlier work. A new venture analysis was conducted in 1978 which addresses a public rather than a private sector business decision (Costello, Posner, Schiffel, Doane, & Bishop, 1978). It is a one-step, detailed analysis of a Go or No Go decision. No preliminary screening steps were included. Figure 2-6 summarizes the approach. Competitive analysis is not addressed by the framework because the decision dealt with an entire industry. Competition from other industries was incorporated into the market analysis through market penetration estimates. The cost estimation was conducted in a manner similar

FIGURE 2-6
Venture Analysis Framework Developed by Costello et al.

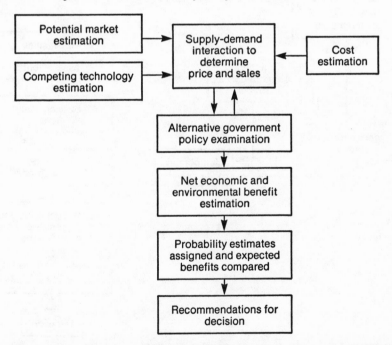

Source: Adapted from D. Costello, D. Posner, D. Schiffel, J. Doaner, and C. Bishop, *Photovoltaic Venture Analysis, Final Report,* 3 vols., SERI/TR-52-040, Solar Energy Research Institute (Washington, D.C.: U.S. Department of Energy, 1978), p. 15, 137.

to the Blackman approach discussed earlier, except it was done at a more aggregated level. Uncertainty is handled explicitly. The decision is viewed independently from other decisions. Therefore, the framework does not consider risk-return trade-offs among alternative new ventures. The approach suffered relative to other frameworks in that key decision makers were not actively involved in the analysis. We will discuss this important factor further in Chapter 11.

Hudson's Framework

Hudson (1977) described a new product decision analysis that was conducted for the Xerox Corporation. The framework, presented in Figure 2–7, is largely oriented toward cost and financial considerations within the firm. Markets are considered but not at the same level

FIGURE 2–7
Hudson's New Product Decision Analysis Framework

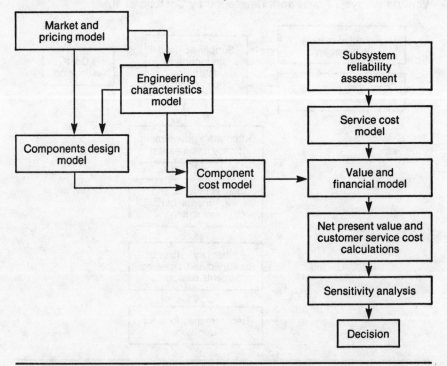

Source: Reprinted by permission of R. G. Hudson et al., "New Product Planning Decision under Uncertainty," Part 2, *Interfaces* 8, no. 1, (November 1977). Copyright 1977 The Institute of Management Sciences.

of detail as the internally controlled factors. The typical net present value and rate of return measures are used to estimate profitability. In a manner similar to Hax and Wiig (1976), uncertainty is explicitly addressed. The approach is not connected to earlier R&D decisions and seems to place very little emphasis on possible competitive reactions. Again, the product decision is analyzed independently from other new venture decisions.

Summary

The new venture decision analysis frameworks that have been developed have many similarities. Each contains investigations of markets or sales potential and the costs of production. These elements are integrated by summary measures of cash flow, usually internal rate of return (IRR) or net present value (NPV). The importance of uncertainty as part of the decision process is usually recognized. It is often treated explicitly. None of the frameworks was designed to sequentially examine research or product development decisions followed by new venture launch decisions. Only Blackman's approach contained a two-step process for screening candidate ideas.

The new venture analysis framework which we have synthesized here is an attempt to overcome the design problems in the existing methods. If implemented correctly, it has the following advantages over existing methods:

1. It explicitly and consistently links the R&D project selection analysis with later new venture analysis.
2. It separates the analysis of market potential from competitive analysis and can investigate specific retaliatory actions of competitors.
3. It can analyze the uncertainty of a new venture from the broader context of the firm's new venture portfolio.
4. It contains methods for generating ideas as well as selecting them.

Each of these potential advantages is only valuable if it can be successfully implemented. The remaining chapters describe specific tools and approaches to make the framework usable in a variety of business circumstances.

3

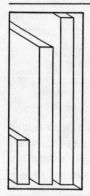

New Venture
Idea Generation

Introduction

New venture idea generation should begin as soon as your corporation has identified a planning gap. Idea generation requires an expansive view of the future needs of consumers and of future technological advances. Creativity is the most important element of the process. Thus, all of the tools to assist in idea generation try to stimulate creativity while subduing the tendency to prejudge ideas or suggestions. Many of the tools presented in this chapter address the psychological barriers to creative thinking. Other techniques use more analytical or mathematically based approaches in an effort to synthesize new ideas, and some combine surveys and expert judgment to forecast technological advances.

The tools to be presented here come from two major sources: market research and technological forecasting. While creative ideas can come from either approach, there is a considerable amount of controversy concerning the relative importance of ideas derived from the two sources. Market research techniques such as consumer focus groups or surveys are the basis for development of many new products. New ventures differ from new products in that they are key strategic actions that the firm considers vital to its long-term existence. New products, on the other hand, serve to sustain or bolster near-term profitability and help to meet the firm's operational or tactical goals. New products are usually extensions or alterations of existing product lines. New ventures have a longer term focus and usually involve a much longer planning horizon than new products. The longer planning horizon, which is associated with larger capital requirements, makes new ventures more uncertain than most new product introductions.

The different nature of new ventures as compared to new product introductions leads some analysts to avoid market research techniques to generate new venture ideas. In an often quoted *Harvard Business Review* article, Abernathy and Kline state that "The argument that no new product ought to be introduced without managers undertaking a market analysis is common sense. But the argument that consumer analyses and formal market surveys should dominate other considerations when allocating resources to product development is untenable" (1980, p. 71). They go on to argue that "Deferring to a market-driven strategy without paying attention to its limitations is, quite possibly, opting for customer satisfaction and lower risk in the short run at the expense of superior products in the future" (1980, p. 71).

The controversy, which has not yet been resolved, highlights the point that the reliance on one type of technique or perspective (for example, customer-generated ideas) can be a major limitation to the creative process. A balanced approach, using numerous techniques and common sense, appears to be the most rational solution.

We will now review a wide variety of idea generation tools, keeping in mind our view that their use brings with it a responsibility not to rely solely on one tool and not to let the tools become a substitute for good managerial judgment.

Technological Forecasting

We will begin our tour through idea generation tools with the work of Wade Blackman. Mr. Blackman (1973) is one of the few analysts who has tried to integrate technological forecasting into the new venture analysis process. As the name implies, technological forecasting is a formal attempt to predict how technologies will develop in the future. It is one way for your firm to gather some information on the future of technology. If your company knew how technology would evolve over the next 10 to 20 years, you could fairly easily generate new venture ideas that would exploit upcoming technologies before your competitors.

Technological forecasting is a combination of analysis and judgment and contains two basic approaches: (1) extrapolating current trends, and (2) obtaining expert judgments. Trend extrapolation can simply extend historical trends in technological evolution, cost declines, or other factors that are significant to your company. At a more systematic level, trend extrapolation can begin with the development of a formal, computer-based model in which relationships between the key factors that will determine the future of those technologies of direct interest to your firm are postulated. The model should include those factors that will cause changes in technological trends. Future values of these causal or secondary factors are then forecasted (extrapolated from past trends). The model can be used to translate predictions based on the causal factors into forecasts of technological trends. This modeling approach may be useful because (1) the causal relationships in the model can be verified or at least discussed, (2) the causal factors may be easier to forecast intuitively, and (3) the historical causal factors may reveal more predictable trends and less volatility.

Building a technological forecasting model that extrapolates current trends into the future is not a simple exercise. Numerous researchers have been searching for the key factors that cause technological changes for many years. The limited success of economists in predicting the future of the U.S. economy vividly demonstrates the problems that can arise. Economic forecasting models can include thousands of causal relationships, require millions of dollars to construct, and still produce unreliable results—even when making predictions as close as 12 to 24 months into the future.

There is a significant challenge to constructing a technological forecasting model for use in new venture idea generation. Your company has a number of options available to meet this challenge. First, another division or group within your company may already have developed a technological forecasting model for other purposes. Your job is to find it, evaluate it, and adapt it to your needs. The second option is to find a related model that is commercially available through, for example, universities, public sector research centers, or consulting firms. The third option is to build your own model or pay outside consultants to build one. The latter option is attractive if you have a relatively good idea of what factors are driving the technologies of interest before the model-building effort begins. The objective of that effort should be to keep the relationships straightforward and the model simple.

A second approach to technological forecasting is to collect expert opinion. Two of the more widely used means of gathering such opinion are Delphi forecasting and cross-impact analysis. These methods do not require the extensive input data and modeling efforts necessary to the building of the trend extrapolation model. The expert opinion-gathering techniques are simpler to implement and usually require fewer resources. Most companies will find them easier to use than formal, trend-extrapolation models.

Delphi Forecasting

Delphi is a technique to help a group of experts reach consensus predictions about future events. (See Linstone & Turoff, 1975, and Sackman, 1975, for good introductions to Delphi forecasting.) A conventional Delphi exercise consists of a series of questionnaires administered to a panel of experts by a smaller group of monitors or researchers.

The first problem you will encounter in conducting a Delphi is the selection of your expert panel. It is important to limit the panel to people with expertise in the technology or industry of interest. Our experience has shown that people are much more likely to agree about future events if they *do not* have expertise in the area at issue. For example, a Delphi panel of experts on energy was assembled as part of a renewable energy study conducted by the Midwest Research Institute (1978). Early rounds of the questionnaire found the group in agreement about future economic conditions (for example, inflation, and gross national product growth rates). However, the group could reach no early consensus on energy demand or supply predictions. Two factors contributed to this situation. First, it was easier for one member to influence the entire panel on nonenergy issues. Second, all the panel members applied similar simplistic rules of logic to reach their predictions on the economy. They appeared unencumbered by the complexities and the past experience of other economic forecasters. As a result, the value of the panel's opinion on the future of the economy was not as useful as its consensus on energy futures. Of course, the latter consensus by this group of energy experts was also much more difficult to obtain.

Once the panel is assembled, they must agree on a relatively broad future scenario. The scenario is designed to ensure that all of the experts base their predictions on the same general set of assumptions about the future. These assumptions may include such diverse factors as political stability, long-term weather conditions, wars, regulations, and laws.

After the general scenario has been agreed on, the first questionnaire is administered. It should contain a substantial amount of data on historical trends of the variables under consideration in order to ensure that all the experts start the process with the same data base. Answers are collected and analyzed for consensus and the results are fed back to the panel along with the second questionnaire. Opinions and justifications for various predictions are also collected, edited, and returned to the group. The analysis and requestioning process continues a number of times until consensus is reached.

The value of Delphi to the new venture idea generation process lies in the interactions and controversies arising in the quest for consensus. The final consensus forecast may be of value, but often it is not. It is the process rather than the end product which is valuable to the venturing company. Conducting a Delphi exercise gives your firm a rare opportunity to hear the opinions of a wide variety of experts outside the company. The opinions aired by the Delphi panel relate directly to the future environment that your business may be facing. The experts have usually had much different training and experiences than your company's management and they are not concerned with the internal issues or culture of your firm.

Before we become infatuated with the benefits of a Delphi exercise, let us review its drawbacks. Delphi has come under considerable criticism from social scientists. For example, Sackman examined the Delphi process and found many weaknesses including:

> considerable evidence that results based on opinions of laymen and "experts" are indistinguishable in most cases; aggregate raw opinion presented as systematic prediction; technical shortcomings, such as untested and uncontrolled halo effects in the application of Delphi questionnaires; unsystematic and nonreplicable definitions, sampling, and use of "experts" manipulated group suggestion rather than real consensus; ambiguity in results stemming from vague questions; acceptance of snap judgments on complex issues; and the virtual absence of a vigorous critical methodological literature even though hundreds of Delphi studies have been published. (Sackman, 1975, p. 3)

Based on his analysis, it is not surprising that Sackman recommended against the use of Delphi. His basic premise for that recommendation is that Delphi has no predictive validity. He does admit that the method has value as an informal exercise for heuristic purposes. New venture idea generation is one of these informal exercises. Delphi, in the context of new venture idea generation, is not required to yield accurate predictions of the future. All that is necessary is that Delphi generate possible futures. A secondary expectation is that the method will provide corporate staff with injections of new thoughts about the future. Delphi thus forces long-term and global thinking that rarely occurs in the daily operations of most corporations. The use of consultants further stimulates the corporate staff to take the Delphi exercises seriously.

Cross-Impact Analysis

Cross-impact analysis is a modification of Delphi that investigates how future events may interact. It does not directly yield new venture ideas. The advantage of cross-impact over Delphi is that it explores interactions of future events in more detail.

One of the many problems with Delphi is that it can easily result in predictions of contradictory events. For example, a Delphi may predict that electric cars will gain popularity and capture 50 percent of the transportation market by the year 2000. At another point in the consensus gathering, the Delphi panel may agree that a new generation steam automobile will be developed. The panel may then predict that sales of steam autos will reach many million per year by the turn of the century. Earlier in the Delphi, the group may have agreed that population growth rates will fall to half their current level by 1995. The summation of these predictions may yield the impossible conclusion that auto sales will exceed transportation demand by a considerable amount. Of course, panel members will identify and avoid obvious inconsistencies.

Cross-impact analysis attempts to systematically eliminate the subtler inconsistencies, and its focus on the interactions of events can also give insights into future technological possibilities and associated risks. A cross-impact analysis was conducted in 1978 on the future of the solar electricity generation industry. Thirty key events were identified that the panel of eight industrial managers agreed were most important to the future of the industry. The timing and cumulative probability of each event were independently estimated, after which the panel estimated the impact of each event on the remaining events. The panel was gathered in the same room and used electronic voting equipment to reach consensus. The cross-impacts and probabilities of independent events were then analyzed by the Monsanto Corporation with the use of a proprietary computer model. The results were (1) identification of reinforcing and inhibiting events, (2) identification of relationships between events that initially appeared unrelated, and (3) indications of the importance of specific events.

In addition to sharing the drawbacks of Delphi discussed above, cross-impact analysis requires more time, resources, and possibly outside consultants. The cross-impact example cited above required three 8- to 10-hour meetings with the panel and about $15,000 (in 1978) for the contractor. However, the benefits of those meetings and intensive discussions were significant. Numerous ideas surfaced concerning key developments that had to occur, critical bottlenecks that would develop as the industry grew, and important actions that the government might take which could help or hurt this emerging industry.

Formal Group Idea Generation Methods

Delphi and cross-impact approaches involve groups that predict future technological events. The predictions can then be used to formulate new venture ideas. Techniques or tools are also available that directly create new venture ideas. These tools include brainstorming, Synectics, and a variation on Delphi.

Brainstorming

Brainstorming is a simple but direct attempt to help people think creatively in a group setting without feeling inhibited or being criticized by others. The rules of a brainstorming session are that each member must build on the ideas offered by the preceding comment. No criticism or disapproving verbal or nonverbal behaviors are allowed. There is often a leader who enforces the rules and records the results. The technique does not require any special expertise by the leader or the participants. (A few practice sessions are usually sufficient to sharpen the leader's skills.) Brainstorming can be used with a wide variety of participants and altered to fit the specific needs of a situation. It is often useful to include representatives of the firm who do not normally interact in the same session. Unlike the conventional Delphi, brainstorming is improved by variety in the participants' backgrounds. If brainstorming sessions are properly controlled by the leader, they can be fun for the participants. Another benefit is that the sessions can help team building within the company. Further descriptions of brainstorming can be found in Urban and Hauser's (1980) book on new product introduction.

Synectics[1]

Synectics differs from other approaches to creative thinking in that it formally deals with the dynamics of the group and also employs strategies to help individuals think in exploratory ways. The steps of a Synectics session are outlined in Figure 3-1. To begin the Synectics session, the problem facing the group is summarized in a simple statement. As the problem owner gives an analysis of the problem, members' desired, wishful outcomes are triggered and given in a form called springboards. The springboards are collected after the analysis and the originator of each springboard gives a brief background of his or her thinking. There is no evaluation.

The function of the springboards is to view the problem from as many different viewpoints as possible. The problem owner then selects one or more of these viewpoints and the group focuses its efforts on developing ideas around the selected springboards. Several strategies to encourage wishful, exploratory thinking may be employed.

When sufficient options are developed, the problem owner again makes a selection of those he or she finds most promising. Each idea is

---

[1] Synectics is the registered trademark of Synectics, Inc., Cambridge, Massachusetts.

FIGURE 3–1
Flow of Synectics Meeting

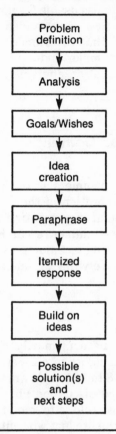

Source: Reproduced with permission of Synectics, Inc., Cambridge, Mass. Synectics is a registered trademark of Synectics, Inc.

then subjected to an open-minded evaluation that identifies both its strengths and those areas where the idea needs further work. The team then develops more ideas, to strengthen the original idea, until the latter is acceptable to the problem owner as a possible solution.

The meeting ends with a listing of possible solutions accompanied by an agenda of action steps for each.

Delphi Variation

The consensus events usually identified in a conventional Delphi are predictions of future events. Delphi can also be used to predict events that are most desired and/or least desired. This Delphi variation was attempted in a survey conducted by M. J. Cetron and D. N. Overly (1973). Their survey, although over a decade old, included several direct new venture ideas. For example, the Delphi variation identified a desire for photochromic glass usable for house glazing by 1985. That desire is a rather explicit new venture idea. One of the most undesirable events identified was that government pollution cleanup policies would bankrupt firms in major industries. Ideas for cost-effective scrubbers and low-cost pollution abatement devices could have been developed instead.

Consumer Needs and Demands Assessments

Direct interaction with consumers is the mainstay of conventional market research. The exploration of the future needs and desires of consumers can also be useful in generating new venture ideas. There are numerous exploratory consumer research methods available. They range from simple questioning techniques to statistically based models of attribute correlations. We will examine a few brief examples that illustrate both extremes.

Focus Groups

Focus groups have been used primarily by market researchers to obtain more qualitative insights into consumers' opinions about specific products. A group of 8 to 10 people are usually gathered together for a relatively open-ended discussion about a product or service. A moderator is present whose role is to keep the group discussing marketing-related aspects of the product without inhibiting the flow of the participants' dialogue. The sessions are recorded or directly observed by management. The results are a set of consumer opinions about the product. The group dynamics are important, as they enable the participants to express thoughts they might not normally verbalize. Examples of focus group interviews in the electric power, automobile air conditioning, and meat product areas are contained in an interesting article by K. K. Cox, J. B. Higginbotham and J. Burton (1976).

As with the Delphi technique, there is controversy about the reproducibility of focus group results, and the ability to generalize the findings to larger groups of consumers. These criticisms may be valid when the objective is to evaluate marketing strategies and customer acceptance. However, when the objective is merely to produce some preliminary ideas for new ventures, they are less valid. The venturing company's management must be aware that ideas generated by market research tools cannot be prevented from being used in further market research once the product(s) is developed. As critics of this technique mention, the fact that one focus group said they would like the product does not mean it will be in demand once it is in production.

Focus group interviews are inexpensive to conduct and can be convened without outside expertise or analysis. Past studies of focus groups indicate that the moderator should have some scientific credentials, but the interviewing technique is not crucial to the success of the interview.

The difficulty with using focus groups for new venture idea generation is that participants may have little or no idea of what their future needs or desires will be. They may not have spent much time thinking about the future and will have little to contribute when the subject arises in the group session. This shortcoming is most devastating to new ventures that require five or more years to reach the commercial production phase. Ideas that could be important in shorter time spans seem well within the cognition of most consumers. This difficulty has led most market researchers to use focus groups as a means of obtaining new ideas for advertising themes, packaging evaluations, and modification to current products.

Focus groups convened to help generate new venture ideas may be limited by a lack of imagination concerning possible future products. On the other hand, the group has a perspective that is so different from that of most technologists that truly unique ideas could arise.

Factor Analysis

Factor analysis (also called perceptual mapping) is at the opposite extreme from focus groups in terms of analytical complexity. It is a mathematical structure, based on linear algebra, which tries to find underlying relationships among a large group of variables. Factor analysis is one technique in the broader field called cluster analysis. Cluster analysis is a procedure for objectively grouping together entities (that is, variables) based on their similarities and differences. Cluster analysis and factor analysis can be conceived as a screen for sifting a large number of seemingly independent variables in an effort to uncover some fundamental, underlying structure. Factor analysis done in the field of market research deals with independent factors that are usually attributes of a product or service. For example, "saves time," "inexpensive," and "solves problems" are attributes that may be used by a consumer to describe a product. Factor analysis takes numerical ratings of products based on each of these attributes and tries to find correlations between them. The correlations indicate more fundamental dimensions on which a product is being evaluated by consumers. For example, using factor analysis, 25 attributes mentioned by a group of consumers could be reduced to two dimensions ("effectiveness" and "ease of use"). Further explanations and examples of factor analysis are given in Urban and Hauser's book (1980) on new product introduction.

Once the fundamental dimensions of a product or service are identified, competing products can be mapped onto the two-dimensional axes. Figure 3–2 reproduces a two-dimensional map of pain relievers developed by Urban and Hauser (1980). The figure shows that all the attributes of nonprescription pain relievers could be factored into the two dimensions of gentleness and effectiveness. The competing pain relievers were then placed into this two-dimensional array based on customer survey results. For example, Excedrin is rated as the most effective but also the least gentle. Tylenol and Bufferin were ranked as about equally effective, but Tylenol was considered gentler.

Displays such as those in the figure can give managers ideas about developing new products that can fill gaps in the alternatives currently facing consumers. For example, if we were interested in a new

FIGURE 3–2
Perceptual Map of Pain Relievers Developed by Urban and Hauser

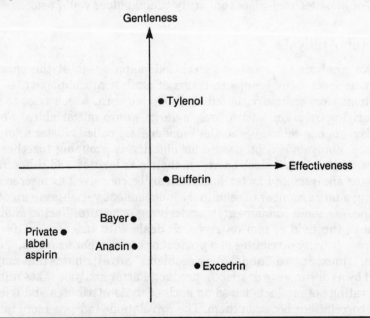

Source: Glen L. Urban and John R. Hauser, *Design and Marketing New Products*, © 1980, p. 187. Reprinted by permission of Prentice-Hall, Inc., Englewood Cliffs, N.J.

venture in the pain reliever market, the key need would appear to be the need for a better combination of effectiveness and gentleness. The nonaspirin-based Tylenol has been successful in its image as a gentler than aspirin alternative. Perhaps another nonaspirin formulation could be developed that would also be perceived as more effective.

Developing maps of fundamental dimensions of products is of obvious value in improving a firm's current product portfolio. The exercise can lead to reformulation of advertising campaigns, new product introductions, or product improvements. Using this technique in order to generate new venture ideas has some positive and some negative aspects. It may be more valid than focus groups in that new venture ideas are derived from fundamental dimensions of current products, rather than by simply asking consumers for new ideas. If these fundamental dimensions are stable, it may be possible to develop a product that is superior to current alternatives. If there are significant technological barriers to developing this superior product, a firm may have to spend a number of years pursuing a new venture with no guarantee that it will capture the market before its competitors.

There are at least four disadvantages to the use of factor analysis for new venture idea generation. First, the detailed statistical analysis may yield dimensions that are already obvious to management, in which case the credibility of the analyst is negatively impacted, and resources are wasted. Second, fundamental features which are important to consumers may change before the new venture reaches the market. Finally, technological improvements unforeseen by consumers may eliminate the entire industry or service under investigation. Alternatively, those advances may enhance the same industry or service. For example, interviews and subsequent factor analysis on slide rule users could have indicated that more easily readable and smaller slide rules were needed. The introduction of low-cost calculators and pocket computers, however, made slide rules curiosities of the past.

The fourth disadvantage is that the amount of data needed to conduct a factor analysis is formidable. The firm's needs for new venture ideas may be better served if the ideas can be appended to a factor analysis presently being undertaken on current products by the firm's marketing department. New venture analysts can either participate in the factor analysis or review the results to help generate needed venture ideas.

Informal Approaches to Idea Generation

A whole array of informal methods of generating new venture ideas exists within a medium- to large-sized corporation. Most of these approaches merely tap the resources already existing within the company. Communication within the corporation and between the company and other organizations is one of the keys to successful new venture idea generation. Some informal approaches to new venture idea generation include:

1. Soliciting ideas from managers and professional staff. These solicitations should be reinforced with individual financial rewards for significant contributions.
2. Monitoring patent filings and inventions.
3. Monitoring trends in technology through trade organizations, professional societies, and universities.
4. Monitoring the introduction of new products by related industries or competitors in your own industry.
5. Establishing periodic meetings of R&D and marketing personnel to exchange ideas about developments and customer needs.
6. Issuing subcontracts to professional consultants to conduct exploratory surveys of technological trends. These organizations can also conduct formal technological forecasting studies or technology assessments.
7. Buying subscriptions to forecasting services or published forecasts (for example, services offered by Chase Econometrics, Wharton, and Data Resources, Inc.).
8. Soliciting ideas from internal R&D staff through requests for research proposals. The proposals should require justification of why the idea can add economic value to the firm.

There have to be substantial monetary and nonmonetary gains associated with these techniques in order to achieve the best employee participation.

A number of other informal approaches could also be developed. Each should be designed to establish a better means of communication between the company and those individuals and groups on the frontier of the industry.

4

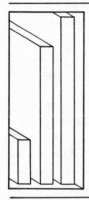

Research and Development Project Selection

Introduction

The initiation of a research project is often the first step in launching your new venture. At other times, a new venture may begin with either a general technological development effort or a more specific product development project. New ventures beginning in any of these three ways face a common set of problems. First, they must successfully accomplish the technical research and development goals that have been established. Second, they must demonstrate more cash generation potential than other investment opportunities to enable the venture to obtain further resources. A well-chosen R&D project portfolio which can overcome these problems will lead to continued future business growth for your company.

The federal government has recognized the importance of R&D in the private sector as well as its role in fostering the economic health of the United States. The Economic Recovery Tax Act of 1981 includes provisions to stimulate R&D investments. A nonrefundable, 25 percent tax credit is allowed on any expansion in a company's R&D expenditures from June 1981 to June 1986. This credit can be taken if a corporation's R&D expenditures are amortized or expensed for tax purposes. A major limitation of the credit is that it can only be applied to increases in R&D expenditures. To determine the amount of the increase, a base period of three years is used. The credit is applied to the difference between the current year's expenses and the average during the base period. A second limitation applies if current year expenses are more than twice the base period average. In that case, the base is adjusted upward to 50 percent of current expenses and the credit is applied. In other words, if a firm's R&D expenses were zero in previous years and $100,000 in the current year, the tax credit would be applicable to only $50,000 and would equal $12,500 ($50,000 × .25).

The stimulation provided by the Economic Recovery Tax Act and the importance of R&D to the future success of many firms are placing added pressure on R&D managers to make well-reasoned decisions. This chapter presents a technique to aid in improving the quality of those decisions.

R&D project selection is a classic example of decision making under uncertainty. In fact, the lack of information about the future potential of research ideas is one of the features that defines research. If there is enough information available to conduct detailed estimates of costs and benefits, the project can no longer be considered at the research stage.

Managers making R&D decisions have to keep two major facts in mind. First, very little information exists on the potential benefits of any alternative research projects under consideration. Second, successful research projects will be reassessed numerous times as they progress toward commercial introduction. The evaluation techniques used to select R&D projects must take these factors into consideration.

The above factors are not the only problems that must be considered when selecting an R&D technique. Numerous authors have outlined other problems and developed models to overcome them. In the following section, we will review those studies. Then, we will combine the insights that we glean with the new venture framework developed in Chapter 2. The approach that results is simpler than most models described in the literature, makes better use of the expertise of various organizational elements within your firm, and does not try to substitute complex calculations for good managerial judgment. The approach has been used at an energy research laboratory. However, many of the same issues must be addressed in any corporate R&D setting.

Review of Research and Development Selection Models

Hundreds of articles have been published on research and development (R&D) project selection models (see Baker & Freeland, 1972, for some examples). The approach which we will present was developed by bringing the best aspects of these previous experiences together. We will begin the discussion of our method by reviewing some of the R&D literature and pointing out the best elements in its approaches.

D. J. Williams

Williams (1969) takes a simple approach to reviewing R&D selection models. He divides all the models into three types, based on the general methods of analysis used. He refers to the first type as the "decision theory" approach. Here, numerous objectives or factors for evaluation are chosen by the decision maker, each of which is given a weight to represent its relative importance in the decision. R&D candidate projects are given a score for each evaluation factor. The scores are weighted according to the relative importance of each factor to the decision maker and then added. The sums are ordered from highest to lowest, and the decision maker picks those projects with the highest score. This approach can be used to produce a very simple or a highly complex version. The key feature in this model is that numerous objectives are simultaneously evaluated.

The second type of model is based on "economic analysis." A single criterion for selection is used: return on investment. The economic benefits of the projects are forecasted along with the associated costs. A present value calculation is made to derive the project's net present value (NPV) or internal rate of return (IRR). Projects are then ranked from highest to lowest NPV or IRR and selected.

The "operational research" approach is the third type of model identified by Williams. This approach attempts to maximize the total value of the R&D project portfolio by using mathematical programming. Numerous constraints on the size and characteristics of the portfolio are specified. Linear programming is then used to maximize total value (a single objective) subject to the constraints.

Williams' review leads him to the conclusion that the "decision theory" approach is best for R&D project selection because numerous objectives can be measured. The use of numerous objectives in an R&D selection model will form the first building block of our R&D selection approach.

W. E. Souder

Souder's review of R&D selection models (1972) tries to empirically assess their usefulness. To accomplish the assessment, Souder uses a decision analysis technique very similar to the one suggested by Williams. Twenty-six R&D administrators/managers were surveyed to determine what properties of R&D selection models are crucial in terms of their usefulness, and the relative importance of each property. The survey indicated that five properties were considered crucial: realism (most important), flexibility, capability, use, and cost (least important).

To measure these five properties, a set of more specific characteristics was developed. These characteristics (shown in Figure 4–1) are more measurable and can be used as surrogates in the scoring system.

Souder's scoring method yields some useful insights into what R&D managers are seeking in selection models. However, the characteristics he uses to measure the five properties limit the approach to an analysis of only computer-based or extremely formal models. Simpler analytical approaches would not receive fair treatment. Nonetheless, the more general properties identified by Souder are important and were kept in mind as we developed our R&D project selection approach.

FIGURE 4–1
Souder's Five R&D Project Selection Criteria and Their Characteristics

1. Realism Criterion Characteristics

Model includes:
Multiple objectives
Multiple constraints
Market risk parameter
Technical risk parameter
Manpower limits parameter
Facility limits parameter
Budget limits parameter
Premises uncertainty parameter

2. Capability Criterion Characteristics

Model performs:
Multiple time period analyses
Optimization analyses
Simulation analyses
Scheduling analyses

3. Flexibility Criterion Characteristics

Model applicable to:
Applied projects
Basic projects
Priority decisions
Termination decisions
Initiation decisions
Budget allocation applications
Project funding applications

4. Use Criterion Characteristics

Model is characterized by:
Familiar variables
Discrete variables
Computer not needed
Special persons not needed
Special interpretation not needed
Low amount of data needed
Easily obtainable data

5. Cost Criterion Characteristics

Model has:
Low set-up costs
Low personnel costs
Low computer time
Low data collection costs

Source: Reprinted by permission of W. E. Souder, "A Scoring Methodology for Assessing Management Science Models," *Management Science* 18, no. 10 (June 1972). Copyright 1972, The Institute of Management Sciences.

N. R. Baker

Baker's article (1974) focuses on the practical application of R&D selection models. He concludes that, although there are numerous models developed, most have not been empirically verified and are not used by R&D managers. Baker discusses some of the more specific problems that face the models. One of the most important is that R&D decisions are made in a hierarchical manner. Each level of management makes budget allocation decisions or subject matter decisions at a different level of aggregation. Given Baker's observation, we believe an R&D selection model must be amenable to hierarchical decisions to be useful.

Baker also points out that R&D project decisions are made more frequently than once a year. They are made continuously, as new ideas are proposed. A selection methodology must be capable of viewing these new ideas as increments in an existing R&D project portfolio.

Another important criticism raised by Baker concerns the treatment of uncertainty: three types are discussed. The first, technical uncertainty, is the risk that the product, process, or device will not work. The second is commercial uncertainty, the risk that the product cannot be economically produced on a commercial scale. The third is economic uncertainty, the risk that after it is introduced the product will not yield economic value to the firm. Baker's article implies that explicit incorporation of each of these three elements of uncertainty into R&D project selection models would be a useful improvement.

M. J. Cooper

A more recent article by M. J. Cooper (1978) reinforces many of Baker's conclusions. Cooper identifies three criteria for selecting research projects: impact, feasibility, and intrinsic scientific merit. Using a weighting system similar to Williams', Cooper develops a simple R&D project selection model based on those three criteria. The impact criterion is measured by the size of the potential market for the product. Feasibility is measured by the probability of achieving certain sales and production cost results. In a manner similar to Baker's, Cooper mentions three types of risks associated with project feasibility: technological risk, technical competence of the research performer, and management capability to accomplish the task. Technological risk defined by Cooper is the same as technical risk defined by Baker. The other two types of risk are quite different from Baker's categories. Part of this difference is explained by Cooper's focus on government research laboratories, as opposed to Baker's emphasis on the private sector.

The final criterion for successful selection mentioned by Cooper is the intrinsic scientific merit of the project. The key question is whether the research contributes to a basic understanding of the phenomena. Cooper argues that this criterion is important because research on the frontier of science keeps highly competent people at the facility and maintains high-quality technical research output. He argues that positive feedback keeps the research quality at a high level. Conducting research at the fringe of current knowledge attracts the best technical people and these people produce the highest quality work. High-quality work attracts more competent people and motivates the existing R&D staff. This phenomenon yields long-term benefits to the company and stimulates all research conducted in the lab.

This last of Cooper's criteria raises an interesting set of behavioral issues about R&D project selection which most authors ignore. His project selection model incorporates this last criterion and the two previous criteria (impact and feasibility) through a simple scoring system. R&D projects are given a ranking for each of the criteria. These rankings are then added to produce a single score for each project. Cooper's treatment of scientific merit and his simple approach to dealing with multiple selection criteria provide additional building blocks for our approach.

M. J. Cetron

Marvin Cetron (1969) attempts, among other things, to review quantitative R&D selection models and develop an improved approach. After an extensive review of existing R&D models, Cetron identifies numerous features that can be used to describe and differentiate between existing models.

As you might expect, none of the existing R&D selection models deals specifically with all the features identified by Cetron. Approaches that possess many of these features will have to be large and complex. If alternative R&D selection models are evaluated with Cetron's criteria, complex, computer-based models have a strong advantage.

Cetron used the results of his review to derive his own R&D project selection model in which complexity is an important element. Figure 4-2 recreates the structure of that model. The structure includes most conceivable aspects of the R&D selection process.

The figure illustrates how a research and development program fits into a broader context of corporate planning and environmental monitoring. The flow of the figure begins on the left side with three overview analyses. Cetron calls these three analyses (a corporate policy review, technology forecasts, and a review of the competitive environment) the "system analysis." The overview of the "system" leads

FIGURE 4–2
Cetron's Framework for Long-Range R&D Planning

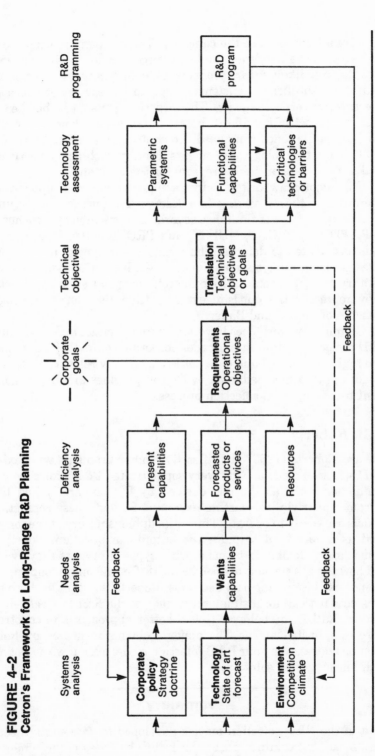

Source: M. J. Cetron, *Technological Forecasting: A Practical Approach*, New York: Gordon Press, 1969, p. 174.

to defining the needs of the company. The company's needs are next compared to the firm's available resources (including its present capabilities and likely future products) to identify any deficiencies. Clarification of the firm's deficiencies lead to a clear set of operational objectives (or corporate goals). The corporate goals must then be translated into a set of specific technical objectives that need to be met. Further details concerning needed technical achievements are identified through technology assessments. Finally, technical objectives are used to formulate an R&D program for the company.

The major drawback of Cetron's approach is that it appears more rigorous than the supporting data deserve. The approach is not unique in its complexity. It is similar to several sophisticated approaches such as PATTERN, PROBE, QUEST, and PROFILE developed for R&D decisions related to defense. These models attempt to use computer-based decision analysis techniques to evaluate the extent to which military R&D projects fulfill numerous national security objectives. They represent the opposite extreme from the simple scoring approaches of Cooper and Baker.

Cetron's approach does have some strong points: It clearly puts the R&D project selection in a broader corporate context. His approach is also highly organized and does not leave out any relevant factors. The breadth of treatment adapted by Cetron provides another key ingredient to an improved selection process.

E. B. Roberts

Edward Roberts (1969) identifies five major problems with existing R&D selection models. First, very sophisticated R&D project selection techniques (such as the one derived by Cetron) are linked to the outcomes of trivial forecasting exercises. Second, these sophisticated models are costly to operate. Third, the dubious nature of the forecasts used as inputs tend to place the outputs in question. Fourth, the models are inflexible in terms of what types of projects they evaluate and how the evaluations are conducted. Fifth, the most troubling, they are not used in managerial decisions. Roberts' solution to these problems does not call for a simpler approach to the R&D project selection process. Rather, he believes that a better approach is to construct a more complicated model. The major problems identified by Roberts must be addressed by our R&D selection model even if we do not agree with his suggested solution.

Summary

Most of the R&D selection models developed to date contain serious drawbacks. Uncertainty about the future business environment and the technical results of R&D projects are the central issues. Some authors have attacked the problem by building more complex models to capture the interactions that influence research outcomes. Others have concluded that the uncertainty cannot be reduced by modeling and have simplified their selection procedures so that they will be better matched to the quality of the existing information.

Our method, presented below, takes the simpler approach to R&D selection. In this respect, it is much like the approaches of Williams and Cooper. Rather than synthesizing better forecasts through modeling, it merely attempts to gather more systematically the existing information from various parts of the organization. It also allows different parts of the organization to assess different apects of R&D risk. Finally, it explicitly includes an evaluation of scientific merit as proposed by Cooper.

A Practical Approach to R&D Project Selection

As mentioned earlier, R&D project selection is often the first step in a broader decision to launch a new venture or introduce a new product. As such, it is sensible to evaluate R&D decisions in a manner consistent with later business decisions. It is also sensible for each subsequent evaluation to build on the information used in these early R&D decisions. Therefore, the method presented below contains many steps similar to those used in most business planning systems.

The approach is summarized in Figure 4-3, which shows the flow of decisions through time and through various management levels. It begins with senior management giving guidance on the priority industries that they want to see the organization enter in the next 10 to 20 years. The problems of defining what constitutes an industry and its boundaries are exactly the same problems confronted by the entire strategic planning function. Any conventions or agreements reached by senior management in the business planning cycle should be used in R&D project selection.

The next step in the approach is for the senior management to rank the priority industries. The ranking can be done in many ways. It may begin with a staff analysis of the attractiveness of alternative industries. On the other hand, the management may feel this issue is one of management philosophy or company tradition. If the style of the senior management team is to share in these decisions, it may be useful for each member to relate his or her personal ranking (with or without the benefit of staff analysis) and then compare it with those of the rest of the group. If the team favors a more democratic process, these rankings can be considered votes. The votes can then be added to

FIGURE 4-3
Major Steps in Our R&D Project Selection Approach

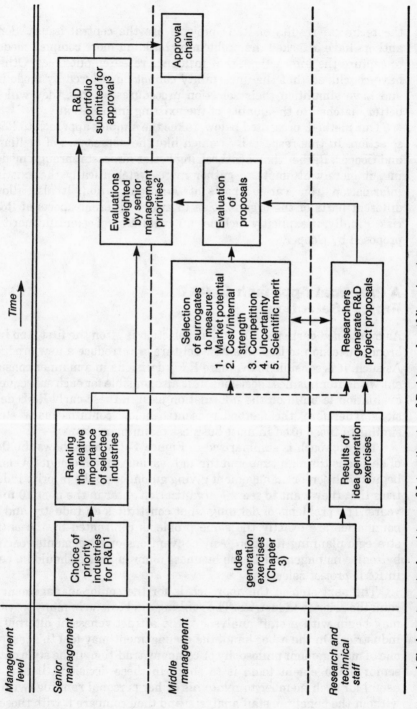

reach a summary ranking. It may also be useful to discuss the rankings and reach a verbal consensus. At the other extreme, the chief executive officer may perform the ranking alone after hearing the suggestions of the senior managers.

An example of these first two steps of the integrated R&D selection approach is provided by recent experience at a large energy laboratory. The senior managers at the laboratory were faced with deciding what R&D areas should receive emphasis over the next five to six years. To make this decision, they first chose 21 areas (or industries) that they considered important. In this example, constraints on the organization's charter required these industries to be selected primarily from the spectrum of renewable energy technologies. This simplified the first step of the selection process for the managers, especially compared with the industry choices facing a larger and more diverse corporation. However, a corporation would probably choose a small number of more broadly defined industries for future emphasis. The 21 separate program areas chosen by the group were then separately ranked by each member of the management team. Most team members had experience in and supervision over only a limited number of program areas. Therefore, it was expected that considerable differences would arise in the ranking. Some differences did arise, although fewer than originally anticipated. The managers involved noted that the exercise was the first time each had explicitly communicated priorities to the others. Although it is impossible to verify, it appears that this communication strengthened the team's commitment to certain programs and helped to nurture a more cooperative atmosphere among the team members.

After the program areas were ranked, each senior manager was asked to rank the importance of various types of research within each program area. The laboratory conducted all types of research from basic research on physical phenomena to economic and social research on customers. Ranking R&D projects required both subject matter (that is, industry selection) and the type of research to be specified. The management team decided to group the various types of research into nine categories:

Basic research.

Applied research.

Exploratory research.

Technology and engineering development.

Economic and social research.

Technology planning and management.

Commercialization planning.

Information dissemination.

Commercialization activities.

The categories chosen highlight the laboratory's focus on the government's role in R&D and technology diffusion. If the laboratory had had a solely private sector focus, the last four activities may have been combined into a marketing function and would probably not be considered part of R&D. Furthermore, the economic and social research category would probably be titled "market research" and would be considered separate from R&D decisions.

The managers ranked the importance of each of these nine categories (by a simple one through nine scale) as they related to each of the 21 program areas. In general, they ranked basic research as the most important research category in those program areas that had not yet been explored. Development and economic research were ranked higher in the program areas closer to commercial viability.

Senior management involvement in the R&D selection process ended with the ranking of industries and the categories of research within each industry. These rankings were given to middle and lower levels of management for decision making on the details of R&D projects.

Returning to the integrated R&D selection approach outlined in Figure 4–3, we see that the next step is to perform a series of analyses on cost, markets, competition, and uncertainty. Middle managers possess the most detailed information on these specific aspects of the company's strengths and competitive position. Therefore, middle managers in different parts of the organization have special expertise in one or more of these areas. Middle managers from the economics/costing and market research departments should evaluate the market potential of the R&D results. The cost analyses should be assessed by marketing and planning groups. Uncertainty measures are derived from the previous analyses and from input by the finance and R&D departments.

One further element must be added to the four analyses outlined above. The success of R&D projects depends critically on the abilities and motivations of the R&D personnel working on the project. As pointed out by Cooper, the scientific merit of the project largely determines the quality of the results and the motivation of the staff. Scientific merit, properly combined with an assessment of the current capabilities of the R&D staff, constitutes an important fifth element of the R&D project selection procedure.

To summarize, once senior management has given general guidance on R&D priorities, middle management should prepare to evaluate R&D proposals in the following areas:

1. Market analysis (to determine the market potential associated with successful commercial development of the R&D idea).
2. Cost analysis (to determine the firm's capabilities with respect to reaching the commercial introduction stage in a competitive cost position.
3. Competitive analysis (to assess the firm's position relative to competitors and the likelihood of securing and maintaining economic value from the idea).
4. Uncertainty analysis (to assess the relative risk of successfully obtaining economic value from the R&D idea compared with competing ideas).
5. Scientific merit (to determine the likelihood of R&D success and its contribution to the quality of the R&D environment in the firm).

Middle managers involved in each of these five analyses may be gathered together using a committee system. As a committee, they will have to agree on some specific criteria to aid in their assessments. For example, managers working on the analysis of scientific merit may choose three or four indicators of merit. These indicators may include staff capability, need for the information by the scientific community, and the contribution to the structure of the lab if the R&D is successful. Once the managers agree on these indicators or surrogate measures, they can rank the projects by the surrogates, apply some type of weighting system, and add them to obtain an overall ranking. The distinction between selecting surrogates and conducting the ranking is seen in Figure 4–3.

Dividing the five analyses among various parts of the organization has several advantages. First, it maximizes the use of expertise and knowledge that is housed in the firm. Because information about the future is scarce, it seems reasonable to focus efforts on collecting available data rather than developing complex R&D selection models that try to generate new information. The latter task has not yet proven to be possible. Second, dividing the analysis forces different parts of the organization to think about the role of R&D in the company's future. The operating divisions may then realize the potential benefits from the R&D group and perhaps provide support for their activities. Finally, dividing the analysis brings managers into contact who do not usually communicate. A coordinator may be needed to ensure that the various inputs are received and processed.

The energy laboratory example cited above can be extended to give further insights into this selection approach. After the senior management ranked the priorities of program areas, approximately 10 to 15 committees were established to select specific R&D projects. Each represented one of the high priority program areas. The committees were chaired and staffed by middle managers. They included representatives from most of the laboratory's organizational divisions. When establishing such committees, managers from R&D, planning, marketing, finance, and operations should be represented. The first job of each committee was to decide what criteria would be used to evaluate the R&D projects. The committee was given the opportunity to choose any evaluation criteria it deemed appropriate. Senior management did not require the committee to use the five types of analyses described above (that is, markets, cost, competition, uncertainty, and scientific merit). As shown in Figure 4–4, the criteria they chose were primarily surrogates for scientific merit. In most settings, use of the broader set of criteria is necessary.

FIGURE 4–4
Sample Criteria Used in R&D Project Selection

Category 1: Staff Capability
One should rank each task in terms of its compatibility with the current staffs' demonstrated expertise, capability, and interest. Specifically, the ranking should include (a) the ability to capitalize on prior or existing research success at the laboratory, (b) current capability and expertise of the staff, and (c) the level of staff interest.

Category 2: Research Needs
One should rank the relative contribution of each task to the direct short- or long-term policy needs of the executive branch and Congress, or indirectly, to the needs of other groups. If the task falls under the program area's first objective, the relevant question is what the probability is that this task will reach a policy-relevant conclusion. If the task falls under the second objective, the question is the probability that this task will produce an advance in the state of the art which will significantly contribute to our ability to achieve the program area's first objective. In either case, evaluators must also consider whether other organizations are already undertaking the same or very similar projects.

Category 3: Contribution to the Laboratory's Stature
In this category, the evaluator should consider the relative contribution of the proposed task toward maintaining and enhancing the laboratory's stature in the planning, analysis, and social science area. One should also consider the likelihood that the project will lead to a new area of activity that falls with the laboratory's mandate but is not yet underway.

Category 4: Government Interest
Each task should be evaluated by the extent to which the government is interested in having our laboratory undertake the task. Those tasks ranking highest in this category should be areas in which that interest has been translated into commitments.

Criteria	Assigned weight
Research need	4
Staff capability	3
Contribution to lab's stature	2
Government interest	1

The committee next applied weights to the four criteria shown in Figure 4–4. The simplest approach to this ranking would have been to assign a number to each criterion, so the most important would receive the highest value. In the example, this ranking would have produced the accompanying results:

Each R&D project proposed would have been assigned a score of one to five for its contribution to each criterion. For example, a score of five for the research need criterion would mean the project fills a very important research need, whereas a score of one would indicate that there is little need for further knowledge in that area.

The scores received for each criterion would then have been multiplied by the weight of that criterion and added across all criteria. This procedure would have yielded a single numerical score which reflected the contribution to the multiple objectives chosen by the committee for each R&D project.

The committee in our example did not follow the most simple approach. The members felt they could provide more information about the relative weights of the criterion. The procedure they adopted is summarized by the evaluation matrix in Figure 4–5. The matrix was constructed by completing the following steps:

1. The committee estimated how many R&D project ideas would be submitted (45 were submitted in our example).
2. They arbitrarily set up a scoring system in which the lowest score was zero and the average score of every cell in the matrix was equal to 5.
3. Given an average score of 5, 45 projects evaluated by 4 criteria would yield a grand total of 900 available points (that is, 4 criteria × 45 projects × 5 points per project per criterion = 900).
4. The committee allocated the total points available (900) to the four criteria (the rows of the matrix in Figure 4–5). In the example, the allocation was research needs = 360 points (40 percent), staff capability = 225 points (25 percent), contribution to laboratory stature = 180 points (20 percent), and customer interest = 135 points (15 percent) (see last column of Figure 4–5).
5. Next, the committee determined the average and maximum number of points that could be given to a single R&D project in its fulfillment of a single criterion. The average number of points per cell in any row of the matrix was simply the total points allocated to the criterion divided by the total number of R&D projects. For example, the average score for evaluating staff capability was 5, which is 225 points divided by 45 projects. The second to last column in Figure 4–5 displays the average for all four criteria. The maximum number of points allocated to a single project in a row of

FIGURE 4–5
Sample Completed R&D Project Selection Matrix

Name of Committee Member: Mr. X

Evaluation criteria	R&D project proposal number												Max. points for a task in this row	Average points for a task in this row	Total points available for this row
	1	2	3	4	5	6	7	41	42	43	44	45			
1. Staff capability	9	9	9	4	5	5	7	8	8	9	5	7	10	5	225
2. Research need	13	10	10	9	6	8	6	10	8	12	5	8	16	8	360
3. Contribution to stature of lab	7	5	7	5	3	5	4	6	4	6	4	5	8	4	180
4. Government interest	4	3	5	6	6	6	3	3	1	6	2	3	6	3	135
Total points of each proposal	33	27	31	24	20	24	20	27	21	33	16	23	—	—	900
Budget estimate is Hi, OK, Lo	OK	OK	Hi	Hi	OK	Lo	OK	OK	Hi	OK	Hi	Hi			

the matrix was simply twice the average. An upper bound was used to prevent any one committee member from placing all his or her available points on a single project in order to assure its selection by the committee.

The system described in these five steps is a zero-sum allocation procedure. The total points available are selected first and the committee's job is to allocate those points across the evaluation criteria (the row totals in the matrix), and then across individual projects (the cells of the matrix). This type of evaluation procedure is quite a bit more challenging and frustrating than a simple ranking. It prevents some committee members from using only the high end of the ranking scale while others are using the lower end. In other words, the system does not allow one member to rank all the projects 4 or 5 (on a 0 to 5 scale) while someone else ranks mostly in the 0 to 3 range. This system mirrors the budget allocation decision that faces senior management.

As shown in Figure 4-3, R&D project proposals may result from idea generation exercises. In our example, these proposals were written by the technical research staff. In order for the committee to conduct a fair evaluation, an equal amount of information on each project had to be provided. Figure 4-6 presents the form used for the R&D proposals. A more detailed project description and budget were prepared for those projects selected by the management.

The final selection of projects in the example was accomplished by adding the committee members' scores and weighting them by the senior management's priorities. The second to last row of the matrix in Figure 4-5 shows the total points given to each R&D project by one committee member. The votes of all committee members were added to obtain an overall ranking. Each of the 45 projects was then placed in one of the general program areas (industries) and one of the nine categories of research that was identified by senior management. The rankings by the senior management were multiplied by the total score received by the project. This multiplication tended to spread the scores over a wider range and give considerable weight to senior management's directions. The total score for a project then consisted of the sum of the rankings by all the committee members times the priority ranking of the area identified by senior management. The system could be used to compare the results in a consistent manner of all committees working on R&D selection and to select all R&D projects for the entire corporation. In our example, the comparison was not done because the system was applied only on a trial basis.

Along with a total score for each R&D project, several other statistics were calculated:

1. The range of points given to each project (the names of the committee members were not attached to their votes).

FIGURE 4–6
Sample Form Used to Submit R&D Proposals to Evaluation Procedure

Proposed R&D Task Title: _____
Author/Principal Investigators: _____
Lead Group: _____
Support Group: _____

Objectives	
Background	
Technical approach	
Expected results	
Funding, personnel, and subcontracting required (in $)	

2. The budget requested by each project (including in-house and subcontracted amounts).
3. Committee members' views of the appropriateness of the R&D project budget (high, low, or OK).
4. A benefit-cost ratio calculated by dividing the total evaluation points received by the project (a measure of its expected benefit) by the total requested budget (in thousands of dollars).

All this information was compiled in a table similar to the example in Figure 4-7 and presented to the committee. Discussion was reopened with the understanding that the chairman had the final decision-making authority. Arguments to move projects up or down in the ranking were heard. (The point rankings already contained general direction from the senior management.) The committee decisions were then sent to senior management for final approval. Senior management reviewed the R&D projects in light of other, ongoing R&D projects at the laboratory. In this sense, the R&D project selection was reviewed as a portfolio.

FIGURE 4-7
Sample Summary Results of R&D Project Evaluation System

Task number	Total points*	Range of points		Budget (in $000s)			Budget evaluation			Benefit cost ratio
		Highest	Lowest	Professional years	Subcontracts	Total	Hi	Ok	Low	
1	324	38	15	150	20	170	2	9	0	1.9
2	306	36	17	97	10	107	0	11	0	2.8
3	317	40	20	80	80	160	0	10	1	2.0
4	322	34	16	162	73	235	7	4	0	1.4
5	240	38	8	195	200	395	6	4	1	.6
6	230	37	9	150	35	185	3	8	0	1.2
7	240	40	10	33	—	33	0	7	2	7.4
. . .										
41	271	37	5	52	0	52	0	10	0	5.2
42	191	26	6	150	50	200	5	5	0	1.0
43	128	21	0	100	0	100	4	5	0	1.3
44	339	40	20	43	50	93	2	7	1	3.6
45	248	29	16	108	15	123	3	6	0	2.0

* The total scores in this example were not multiplied by the senior management rankings because they all fell into a single research area and program.

Conclusions

The real test of any R&D selection model is whether it is used in decision making. The energy laboratory discussed in this chapter did use the approach to aid in project selection on a trial basis. The entire selection procedure took about two weeks to complete. The meetings took a substantial percentage of the total time required, with most of the time (in and out of meetings) spent seriously considering the strengths and weaknesses of each proposal. The mechanics of the process were conducted by clerical staff. Most participants felt the procedure was useful and that the time commitment was reasonable relative to the importance of the decisions. The process led to a stronger commitment to research projects selected and also highlighted important differences in alternative research proposals. The simplicity of the approach allowed it to be quickly accepted and added credibility to the exercise.

5

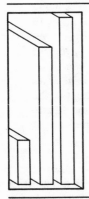

New Venture
Analysis:
Markets

Introduction

In Chapter 2, we made a distinction between analyses required to select an R&D project and analyses that precede the launching of a new venture. This chapter is the first of five that deals with the second group of analyses. Before a major capital commitment is made to a new venture, four types of analyses must be completed. They are: (1) analysis of market potential, (2) examination of the expected competition for given markets, (3) analysis of cost trends over time, and (4) an assessment of the relative uncertainty of the venture. Chapters 5 through 8, respectively, deal with each of these analyses. The four analyses must then be combined so that their interaction can be examined and a decision on the new venture can be reached. The latter task is the subject of Chapter 9.

Market analysis has to be the single most important element of the new venture analysis. If market potential is large enough, it can overshadow many cost problems, competitor threats, or the other financial risks. Unfortunately, market potential is also the hardest analytic task facing a new venture. Countless numbers of start-up companies have failed and even more have never obtained original financing because of insufficient attention to an understanding of market potential. A new venture within an existing firm faces the same threat.

There are at least two causes for inadequate assessment of market potential. Probably the most common cause is a belief that the market is too large to even bother analyzing. An example of that line of reasoning would be the following:

> Our new venture will produce an electronic car maintenance sensing system. It will fit all late-model, U.S. domestic automobiles and will cost $600. We know that there were 6,375,506 passenger cars produced in the United States in 1980. The 1981 production level was 6,253,138. Our market potential is $7.6 billion for those two years alone! If we get only 1 percent of that market, we will still have sales of $76 million. Furthermore, we have purposely underestimated the total size of the market (that is, excluded 1982, 1983, and future years). Therefore, our sales will be near $100 million, even if we get .5 percent rather than 1 percent market share.

The second major cause for inadequate market assessment is a frustration about the uncertainty of future markets. This is most often manifest in statements concerning the validity of your "gut feel" for markets. The argument begins with the assertion that market analysis is never successful in predicting major innovations or changes. An example often cited is the inability of U.S automobile manufacturers to foresee the changing energy situation and the increased demand for smaller cars. Given that market analysis is futile, the argument continues, the new venture manager is left with only his or her intuition about future market trends on which to base judgments.

Both of these reasons for not conducting adequate market research seem weak at best. Experienced venture capitalists are skilled at spotting inadequate market assessments and at showing their displeasure strongly (usually by denying funds to the venture or by not reading the rest of the new company's business plan). The new venture management team within an established corporation must also be aware of this problem.

This chapter begins with the assumption that market analysis can provide useful insights. It recognizes that realizing this potential is difficult and requires artful application of the available tools. At a minimum, market analysis provides a framework for learning more about the market and offers the discipline necessary to investigate all relevant market issues.

The objectives of a market analysis should be (1) to determine the potential size of the market over time, and (2) to estimate how quickly the market will adopt your new product or technology (resulting in a forecast of total annual sales). This chapter reviews various approaches to meeting both of these objectives. The first section addresses the issue of potential market size; the second examines the rate of new product adoption.

The distinction between estimating total market potential and annual industry sales can be seen as analogous to separating rational needs from the actual behavior of individuals. Total market potential can be defined as the upper limit of an industry's annual sales; that is, the total number of sales that would occur if all decisions were based on the life-cycle cost of the new product relative to the next best existing alternative—assuming all consumers had perfect information and infinite supplies of the product. Hence, market potential would equal annual industry sales in a world of perfect markets and no transaction costs.

Estimates of total annual sales, on the other hand, try to take market imperfections and transaction costs into account. Rational and irrational buyer actions are estimated (at least at an aggregate level). In the second section of this chapter, we will also address some persistent trends in the behavior of buyers when they are faced with a new technology or product. These trends are often used as the basis for estimating annual industry sales.

As mentioned earlier, predicting future potential markets and future industry sales is an uncertain activity even if analytical tools are used. Separating potential market size from estimated annual sales makes the analyst's job easier primarily because it allows him or her to take advantage of the limited available knowledge. This is one way of instilling discipline into the market assessment task.

Table 5-1 gives an example of the degree of uncertainty present in the early phases of a new venture analysis. The table shows six independent estimates of the future sales of solar heating and cooling systems in the United States in 1980, 1985, and 1990. Four of the studies were completed in 1974, one in 1976, and one in 1977. Each was done by a reputable company or task force of experts using state-of-the-art analytical techniques. It is probably safe to assume that more resources were dedicated to the development of these estimates than to most private industrial estimates conducted over the same period. The last line of the table shows the actual sales in 1980 as estimated by Arthur D. Little, Inc. in March 1981.

The table graphically illustrates uncertainty in at least three distinct ways. First, the a priori estimates for 1980 sales range from 0.7 trillion to 27.0 trillion Btus. Second, the later predictions of solar penetration (1976 and 1977) do not seem superior to estimates made in 1974. Third, knowledge of the actual 1980 sales is limited and is subject to a significant range of uncertainty.

Results such as those shown in Table 5-1 make it more understandable why some new venture managers would rather rely only on intuition. The figures indicate that (1) analytical approaches to new venture markets will always be inaccurate, (2) it is easy to overvalue

TABLE 5-1
Estimates of Solar Heating and Cooling of Buildings: Utilization versus Actual Results (btu × 10^{12}/year—energy produced)

	1980	1985	1990
Project Independence Solar Task Force (1974)[a]			
Business-as-usual, oil $11/barrel	11.7	280	550
Arthur D. Little, Inc. (1976)[b]			
Business-as-usual	21.3	38.0	56.7
Mitre/METREK Corporation (1977)[c]			
Base case	.7	7	33
General Electric (Phase 0 1974)[d]			
New construction applications	10	80	190
Westinghouse (phase 0 1974)[e]			
Capture potential	6	28	41
TRW Systems Group (Phase 0 1974)[f]			
Low-level estimate	27	—	406
Actual energy produced[g]	1–5	—	—

[a] "Project Independence, Final Task Force Report, Solar Energy." Prepared by NSF for FEA (with technical inputs from A. D. Little, Inc.), November 1974, pp. 11–39.

[b] A. D. Little, Inc., "An Analysis of the Market Development of Dispersed Usage Solar Energy Systems: 1976–1990." Draft Report to FEA, March 1976, pp. 11–78. The same projections were used as a base for the FEA *National Energy Outlook,* March 1976.

[c] As described in Bezdek et al., "Detailed Analysis of Policy Options for Accelerating Commercialization of Solar Heating and Cooling Systems," Washington, D.C.: The George Washington University, April 1977.

[d] General Electric Co., Solar Heating and Cooling of Buildings, Phase 0, Space Division, NSF-RA-N-74-021, May 1974.

[e] Westinghouse Electric Corp., Solar Heating and Cooling of Buildings, Phase 0, Special Systems, NSF-RA-N-74-022, May 1974.

[f] TRW Systems Group, Solar Heating and Cooling of Buildings, Phase 0, NSF-RA-N-74-023, May 31, 1974.

[g] Arthur D. Little, Inc., estimate, personal communications, March 1981.

Source: Midwest Research Institute, Solar Heating and Cooling of Buildings (SHACOB) Commercialization Report, Part A (Kansas City, Mo.: U.S. Department of Energy, 1978), p. 88, with additions.

the results merely because they had an analytical basis, and (3) analysis still provides more insight than would be obtained from intuition or back-of-the-envelope calculations. With these limitations clearly in mind, let us examine the available tools for the task.

Forecasting Market Potential

Estimating the total size of the market for a new service, product, or process has to take advantage of whatever information and insights are currently available. Relevant information usually includes trends in historical data and relationships that appear to be stable over time. Insights can be obtained from experts in the field, researchers, and managers who participate in current market events. The job of the analyst at this stage of the new venture is to obtain all the available information and insights and translate them into a forecast of market potential.

The most common approach to forecasting market potential is the development of scenarios. We have also developed our own method which, for lack of a better term, we have called *needs assessment*. A third method is to use whatever combination of informal techniques is appropriate in a specific circumstance. We will discuss both the formal and informal methods in the sections that follow.

Scenario Development

A scenario can be defined as a statement of possible future events which, at least in the view of the scenario writer, are internally consistent. Scenario writing is similar to historical writing except that, rather than recording past events, it deals with projections about the future. Major events are highlighted along with their predicted dates of occurrence. Reasons for these events are given, as are their ramifications for other future events. Techniques such as time lines and written statements are used to document the scenario formulation. Scenarios do not have to reflect the most likely future. They are only expected to make plausible and internally consistent predictions. When predicting future market size, the scenario writer usually includes estimates of this kind of potential as part of his or her final product.

The development of scenarios can take a wide variety of forms. Managers or analysts can compose them simply because they are a job requirement. This approach is used by at least one major energy corporation we contacted. The scenario developer may choose to construct a scenario in a more systematic way. (Many systems are available.) Blackman (1973) provides a simple framework for constructing scenarios (see Figure 5-1). He suggests forecasting the technological, economic, ecological, sociological, and political environments separately, and later combining them into a complete scenario of the future. The result will be a scenario that is more comprehensive in its treatment of factors influencing market potential.

Blackman refers the reader to a whole set of forecasting techniques (primarily from the field of technological forecasting) that can be used to examine each of the five environments depicted in the figure. He warns that the most useful techniques will depend on the particular

FIGURE 5–1
Blackman's Framework for Scenario Development

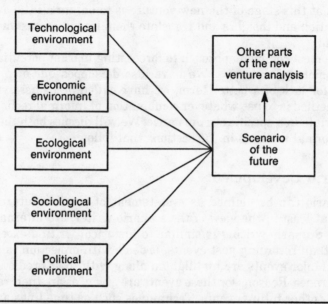

Source: Reprinted by permission of the publisher from "New Venture Planning: The Role of Technological Forecasting," by Wade Blackman, *Technological Forecasting and Social Change* 5, pp. 25–49. Copyright 1973 by Elsevier Science Publishing Co., Inc.

market or new venture that is being examined. Some of the tools include:

Delphi and cross-impact analyses (discussed earlier).

Substitution curves (see below).

Dynamic modeling.

Trend extrapolations.

Quantified analogies.

A good introduction to these tools and examples of their applications are provided by Jones and Twiss (1978), Cetron (1969), and Ayres (1969).

In most applications, at least three alternative scenarios are developed. The first is a surprise-free future, which serves as a baseline. The second and third alternatives usually include some likely changes in the environment such as slow and rapid economic growth, or a fixed state of technology and a rapidly changing technical base. Jones and Twiss (1978) provide some step-by-step guidelines for scenario writing.

They also review examples of how scenario writing has been conducted at General Electric and at Shell Oil.

Needs Assessment

Sometimes the new venture analyst is faced with the fortunate situation of having access to other people's forecasts. These forecasts are most likely to take the form of publically available information concerning energy use, macroeconomic activity, population growth, and/or other demographic or economic statistics. These statistics can be combined to get an estimate of the aggregate future demand for a generic type of service (for example, electrical energy, housing, or transportation demand). The use of other forecasts to predict market potential is termed a *needs assessment*. It is often possible to predict cost trends for existing products or services that are designed to fill that demand. Even limited knowledge of the future costs of a new venture may allow one to estimate its potential market. Figure 5-2 presents the technique of needs assessment in the form of a flowchart accompanied by potential sources of information.

We will examine this flowchart with the aid of an example. Recently, we conducted a market analysis on a renewable electric energy technology. Consulting firms, econometric forecasting firms, and forecasts available in the literature formed the basis needed to estimate aggregate demand in this situation. It was necessary that we estimate the aggregate demand for electrical energy in U.S. households. We were able to find a considerable amount of information and many forecasts on the future electricity needs of the household, industrial, and commercial sectors. Trend extrapolation may be a good source of projections in many settings. However, the series of energy crises beginning in 1973 made the use of this technique dubious with respect to energy forecasting. We therefore relied on published forecasts rather than extrapolations in our example.

After aggregate demand is forecasted, prices of the conventional products and the new venture's product are calculated simultaneously (see Figure 5-2). We must point out that this price analysis differs from the cost analysis we will discuss in Chapter 7. The latter takes the perspective of the buyer and compares his or her alternatives in order to fulfill the stated demand. The comparison of prices (usually including the present value of after-tax maintenance and operating costs over the life of the product) is used to calculate the potential market available to the new venture. You can do the calculation in' several ways. The price of conventional products can be estimated as a single value or as a range of possible prices with an associated probability distribution. The price distribution curve represents differences

**FIGURE 5-2
Suggested Structure for Estimating Market Potential Using Needs Assessment**

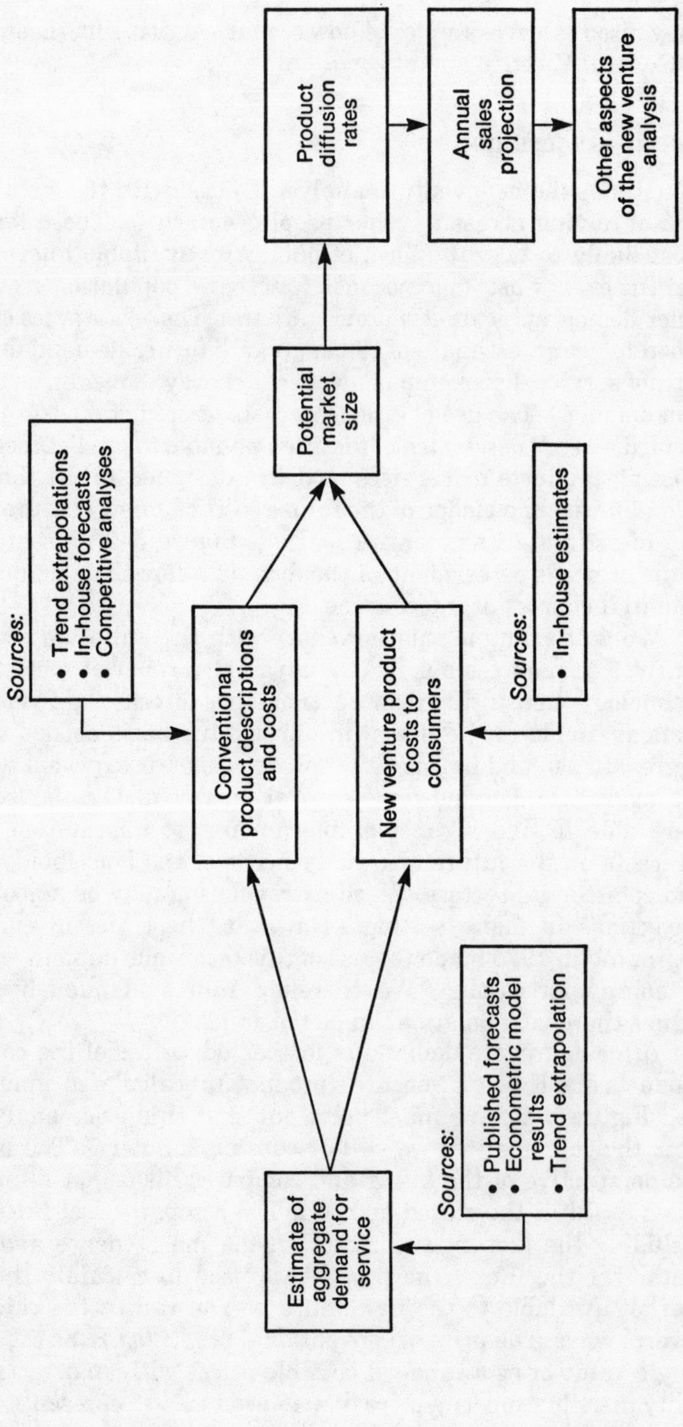

Sources:
• Trend extrapolations
• In-house forecasts
• Competitive analyses

Conventional product descriptions and costs

Sources:
• In-house estimates

New venture product costs to consumers

Potential market size

Product diffusion rates

Annual sales projection

Other aspects of the new venture analysis

Estimate of aggregate demand for service

Sources:
• Published forecasts
• Econometric model results
• Trend extrapolation

in geography, product features, and manufacturers of the product. You can also display the price of the new venture product as a single value or as a probability distribution. Market potential is then some fraction of the new product's total demand based on the probability that the product's price will be equal to or less than the price of conventional alternatives. In our example, the price distribution of renewable electric energy systems was compared to the distribution of conventional electric utility rates. This comparison would lead, for example, to a conclusion that the renewable technology is likely to be priced lower than conventional alternatives in 1 to 2 percent of all U.S. households. If we had kept the analysis on a national basis, we would estimate the total market potential to be 1 to 2 percent of the total U.S. housing stock. However, we were not satisfied with estimating market potential only on a national basis.

Data at the state and standard metropolitan statistical areas (SMSA) was more appropriate. The distribution of the prices of the renewable energy systems was based on a number of key constraints that the technology faced. For example, aerial surveys had been conducted on sample communities to estimate the number of single family homes with adequate roof areas and the correct physical orientation for installation of the energy system. Multifamily dwelling surveys had to consider the number of units in the building as well as orientation and available area for installation of collectors (including roofs and parking structures). The price of the technology would be very high in those buildings that were not suited for the latter installation. The price distributions used to estimate market potential were therefore skewed by those physical constraints.

The remainder of the flowchart in Figure 5-2 shows the relationship between the market potential estimate and other elements of a new venture analysis. We will discuss the translation of market potential into annual sales estimates in the next section. The integration of the sales estimate into the other parts of the new venture analysis will be the subject of Chapter 9.

A needs assessment differs from scenario development in that it depends more on information generated outside the company rather than on the creative thinking of company managers. It is basically a synthesis of existing forecasts to fill the needs of the new venture and may appear to have more validity than internally generated scenarios. However, managers should seriously question this conclusion in each circumstance because the analyst may merely be substituting the uninformed guesses of a third party for internally generated guesses. Stated differently, the fact that the forecast can be referenced in published literature, government reports, or consulting firm reports is of only limited usefulness to the new venture.

Informal Market Penetration Approaches

We have noticed some interesting trends in our estimation of the market potential of all types of products and technologies. Almost every market assessment begins by using informal approaches. The task usually starts with all the analysts or managers involved doing some relatively random literature searches. Libraries, and reference librarians in particular, can be major assets at this point. The most useful sources of information depend on which markets are of interest. Many investment banks and brokerage houses, for example, publish reports on selected markets and competitors in those markets. These reports represent the results of rather extensive market research. Trends in technologies and tastes are usually identified and the strategies of key competitors are explained. These reports can be very helpful when conducting the competitor analysis (see Chapter 6).

A second useful source of information is government-funded market studies. These can be found by using the National Technical Information Service (NTIS) or through calls to relevant government agencies (for example, the Department of Energy, Department of Transportation, or Department of Commerce). Such calls can often reveal studies not yet in the NTIS or those never entered into the NTIS system. Ongoing studies can also be identified in this manner. The names of university or other researchers working in the field of interest can also be obtained from government agencies

Do not forget that state and local governments spend a considerable amount of money doing market research. Data from these sources tends to be much more detailed than national data. If two or more states have conducted similar market research, the results may allow you to extrapolate the trends to a national level, or at least provide some insights into the national data.

Consulting firms are constantly conducting market studies for specific clients or for wider sale. For example, Frost and Sullivan, Inc. sells market research reports covering numerous markets in the United States, Europe, and the rest of the world. The studies cost between $900 and $1,700. They are often quite specific and can be very valuable if they address the market that your new venture will enter.

Computer-based data bases are another good starting point. Several indexes of business periodicals are accessible through on-line computer services. The searches can usually be done by subject area. Some on-line services abstract the articles as well as giving the complete reference. We find these abstracts of special interest because they obviate the need to hunt through all types of publications to learn the contents of relevant articles.

After these initial assaults on the market are completed, a period of regrouping usually occurs. At this point, we have often turned to structuring scenarios or initiating a needs assessment. Under other circumstances, continuation of informal market research techniques is appropriate.

A good example of how an informal research approach can yield market potential is one we completed in late 1982. The market of interest was small hospitals (less than 200 beds). The new venture dealt with the application of minicomputers and micro-computers to that market. The initial review of the literature yielded two key facts. First, detailed statistics were available on hospitals in the United States including size, location, and services offered. Second, rising costs and increasing competition in the health care industry were reducing the number of small hospitals in the United States. The next step in the market analysis then became clear. Gathering data on the number of small hospitals currently operating and the trend in the last decade became our first priority. Medical libraries and trade associations were able to provide those data. Our second effort was to determine how these institutions were currently meeting their data processing needs. That search led us to the staffs of selected trade associations and to the publishers of specialized trade magazines. For example, Cardiff Publishing Company publishes a monthly magazine entitled *Computers in Health Care*. Their marketing staff had conducted surveys that were useful to our purpose. In addition, our inquiries did not pose a competitive threat to the organizations that had the relevant data.

The results of our informal market analysis yielded defensible market potential forecasts. Formal scenario development or needs assessments were not necessary. If the same approach had been applied to the delivery of home health care (a growing substitute for hospital-base care), the scenario development approach may have been superior.

Each market potential estimation task must be considered unique. The method of market assessment is best if it evolves as the circumstances dictate. Assessing market potential will undoubtedly remain more of an art form (or craft) than a scientific process for the foreseeable future.

Forecasting Future Sales

Market potential estimates have to be modified to yield forecasts of company sales. Market imperfections and "less-than-cost-rational" behavior of purchasers are two reasons why potential and actual sales always differ. In fact, the largest number of uncertainties in estimating the future market penetration of a new product may arise from predicting the behavior of the individuals who comprise the identified potential markets. As we described in the previous section, predicting the size of the potential market is also difficult. However, it may be possible to rely on ongoing, long-term trends in markets and analytical tools that predict future changes based on historical or observed relationships. To accurately predict the sales of a new technology or product, we must understand how individuals, corporations, or other prospective buyers make decisions. One important factor, which plays a role in many decisions, is the relative price of competing products. Comparative prices are certainly not the only decision criteria. In some product decisions, price plays little or no role. Examples can also be found of products whose demand seems to increase as the price rises. "Snob appeal" products fall into this category. Therefore, prediction of new product sales based on comparative prices alone certainly will lead to inaccuracies. You will notice that even our comparison of prices in the earlier needs assessment did not use simple stated prices as the basis for market potential. When market potential is translated into sales forecasts, dependence on comparative prices becomes even more risky.

The other factors that affect the purchaser's decisions are not easy to identify on an aggregate level and are difficult to integrate into a predictive model. The types of decision factors involved and their relative importance may also change as one moves across market sectors, or they may change over time. The lack of knowledge about how purchase decisions are made must be kept in mind as we predict sales. All sales forecasts are therefore subject to considerable uncertainty and should be used with caution.

We have identified two general approaches to translating market potential into sales forecasts. The first draws on observation of historical innovations and their behavior in the marketplace. The second is again an informal and heuristic approach that can sometimes be used.

Forecasting Innovation Diffusion Rates

In this world of imperfect knowledge about purchase decisions, there are few stable behavior patterns to aid the new venture analyst. One exception is the pattern with respect to how one product penetrates a market over time. Historic substitutions of one technology for another have tended to follow a pattern shown by an S-shaped substitution curve. This pattern has been observed in dozens of cases ranging from new steel production technologies to markets for new consumer products.

In intuitive terms, the S-shaped pattern begins with a period of very low sales that increase at a slow rate. This is the period in which innovative customers are trying the product or technology. The product's appeal at this point is probably its unique technical qualities or merely its curiosity value. Economics usually plays a negligible role in the purchase decision at this point. The second phase of the market penetration pattern is a period of rapid and increasing sales growth and expansion. By this stage, there is a general awareness of the product in the marketplace. Its purchasers are generally the more innovative half of the majority of consumers. Economics will often become the key driving force behind the purchase decision during this phase.

The third phase of the penetration pattern is continued expansion of sales but at a slower rate. Purchasers in this phase are similar to those in the previous stage but less innovative. The factors influencing the purchase decision of this later group are similar to those that motivated the earlier purchasers. The final phase of penetration is decreasing sales as the market reaches saturation. Sales at this point will be attributed to replacement and there will be only a few new customers.

Unfortunately, the time required for the substitution process to occur has not shown any stable pattern. The time required for a product's market penetration to increase from 10 percent to 90 percent is commonly termed *takeover time*. Table 5-2 lists takeover times for

---

TABLE 5–2
Logistic Substitution Model and Examples of Takeover Times for New Products

Substitution	Takeover time (years)
Synthetic/natural rubber	58
Synthetic/natural fibers	58
Plastic/natural leather	57
Margarine/butter	56
Electric arc/open hearth specialty steels	47
Water-based/oil-based paint remover	43
Open hearth/bessemer steel	42
Sulfate/tree-tapped turpentine	42
Plastic/hardwood residence floors	25
Plastic/other—pleasure boat hulls	20
Organic/inorganic insecticides	19
Synthetic/natural tire fibers	17.50
Plastics/metal—cars	16
BOF/open hearth—steels	10.50
Detergent/natural soap (U.S.)	8.75
Detergent/natural soap (Japan)	8.25

Source: Reprinted by permission of the publisher from "A Simple Substitution Model of Technological Change," by J. C. Fisher and R. H. Pry, *Technological Forecasting and Social Change* 3. Copyright 1971 by Elsevier Science Publishing Co., Inc.

16 different products. The takeover times in the figure ranged from 8.25 years to 58 years. Figure 5-3 provides a graphic display of results for three historical substitutions. All show the S-shaped substitution curve but each has a different time scale.

The basic S-shaped product substitution curve has been examined by numerous authors (see, for example, Blackman, 1971, Fisher and Pry, 1971, Lenz and Lanford, 1972, and Mansfield, 1961.) The model has been applied to broad categories such as the substitution of synthetic for natural fiber. It has also been applied to more clearly defined products such as the substitution of synthetic for natural fibers in tires. Various authors claim that such a model can be applied once an ongoing substitution is 2 to 10 percent complete. However, significant errors are often found in the results of such projections. The lack of any consistent explanation for how long the process will take is one of the major contributors to such errors.

It is even more difficult to apply such a model to a new venture when initial penetration of major markets has yet to occur. Thus, historical data is not usually available to define (1) the time of initial market penetration, and (2) the likely takeover time once penetration begins.

Some authors have tried to overcome the more obvious shortcomings of the substitution curve by adding variations. For example, in the absence of historical data, techniques have been developed to estimate the key parameters of the curve. Blackman (1971) and Mansfield (1961) have determined that the relative profitability of the new technology, compared to industry standards and the tendency of an industry to innovate, are two key variables influencing the rate of product or technology substitution. Blackman's formulation of the penetration curve relates market penetration at any point in time to an index of the industry's potential for innovation, the profitability of the new product, and an index of the product's initial cost. Innovation indexes for selected industries are shown in Table 5-3. The value of the index for each industry is not important to our discussion except that it shows the relative innovation potential of the industries listed. Such a model has been used to project the rate of market acceptance prior to the introduction of a new product. One of the key judgmental aspects of the approach is to determine the appropriate values entering the model. This is done by using data from prior technology substitutions. The selection of the appropriate prior substitution is both subjective and crucial to the model results.

Blackman's variation on the basic substitution curve has some obvious advantages. It also has at least one problem. The Blackman model does not take into account temporal changes in the economic feasibility of the new product relative to the conventional alternatives.

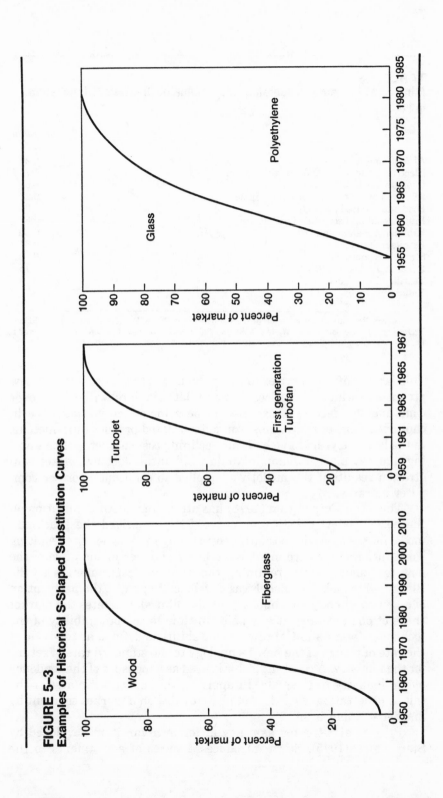

FIGURE 5-3
Examples of Historical S-Shaped Substitution Curves

TABLE 5–3
Ranking of Industries According to the Value of Blackman's Innovation Index

Industry	Innovation index
Aircraft and missiles	2.29
Electrical machinery and communication	1.76
Chemicals and allied products	0.60
Auto and other transportation equipment	0.29
Food and kindred products	−0.35
Professional and scientific instruments	−0.37
Fabricated metals and ordinance	−0.60
Petroleum products	−0.64
Stone, clay, and glass	−0.70
Paper and allied products	−0.75
Textile mill products and apparel	−0.75
Rubber products	−0.76

Source: Reprinted by permission of the publisher from "New Venture Planning: The Role of Technological Forecasting," by Wade Blackman, *Technological Forecasting and Social Change* 5, pp. 25–49. Copyright 1973 by Elsevier Science Publishing Co., Inc.

This is a significant barrier to using the model to project sales for new products in which unit prices (in noninflated dollars) will decline over time and the decline is expected to be a major motivating force in capturing market share. Most computer-related product introductions in the last five years have had this declining cost characteristic. Ignoring that key market dynamic would yield unsatisfactory market penetration results if the model was applied to semiconductors or computer markets.

The BDM Corporation (1978) has attempted another variation on the basic product substitution curve. They rederived the Blackman model for the case where relative costs change over time. The resulting substitution curve accounts for the latter changes in the price of the new technology, while retaining the same basic parameters as the Blackman model. The model was developed to predict the penetration of a new solar energy technology (photovoltaics). It relates the market share of photovoltaics at any point in time to the profitability of the technology and its initial price. Profitability is defined as the ratio of the rate of return of the new technology to the standard rate of return for the industry. A constant factor is used as a measure of the tendency of the industry to innovate. In applying the model, estimates of the initial penetration levels have to be provided on a market segment by market segment basis.

Price is also treated as a key factor in a variation developed by Stern et al. (1975). Stern introduces a series of adjustments to the relative price of the competing technologies. These adjustments allow the analyst to explicitly incorporate the effects of a variety of product attributes on the sales forecast. This capability is appealing from a methodological point of view but requires a great deal of subjective judgment concerning which product attributes will affect consumers (and to what extent).

Informal Approaches to Sales Forecasting

The process of estimating market potential can sometimes yield ideas on how to forecast sales. This occurs most frequently when the new technology or product being considered is very large or expensive and the number of customers is limited. Under these conditions, it is possible to forecast individual sales and then aggregate the results to produce a total sales forecast.

Let us return to the health care (small hospitals/computers) example to illustrate this process. The new venture management team originally believed that their product was a high-technology computer with state-of-the-art software. After the market potential investigation, the team began to realize that they were offering a labor-intensive service to these hospitals. They needed a substantial sales and service force to gain and sustain market share.

The sales estimate for this new venture began with a tabulation of the small hospitals (and related health delivery organizations) within geographic proximity to the company's headquarters. Research was conducted to determine how many sales calls were typically required and what the lag was between initial customer contact and the sale. The institutions involved typically required meetings of their board of directors before making capital expenditures. This factor slowed the decision process by many months. After gathering as much data on customers' decision processes as possible, the new venture analysts made judgments on the average sales call success rate, the average lag before a sale, and the number of sales calls possible per week of sales effort. These factors were then used to determine allocation of sales calls among the states in the new venture's original marketing territory. A simple equation, which multiplied success rates times the number of calls times the number of hospitals in each state (plus an adjustment for the lag), allowed annual sales per state to be forecasted. The product-substitution model concept was used to change the rate of sales call successes over time (producing an S-shaped sales forecast).

The effort expended on the small hospital sales forecast bore fruit in numerous ways. First, the forecast had credibility because its derivation was logical, easy to follow, and included the key determinants of sales. Second, it dictated how many salespeople and what travel expenses would be needed to achieve the sales goals. The venture had a mechanism to directly link sales forecasts to crucial cost elements (sales and administrative expenses). A general indication of how quickly the sales force had to be hired also resulted. In addition, the number of service personnel needed to support the forecasted sales levels could be estimated. Finally, the entire sales forecasting model was constructed on a personal computer using electronic spreadsheet software. Thereafter, scenario and sensitivity analyses became easy to conduct.

Informal approaches to sales forecasting have to evolve as market information arises. Such approaches can use concepts from the product substitution model or from other methods discussed here. The innovativeness of the new venture team remains key to producing credible sales forecasts for the venture.

Summary

The techniques used most frequently to predict sales have been based on either the S-shaped substitution curve or on informal approaches without any theoretical underpinnings. Realizing that the market penetration curve represents only an observation with no causal foundation, researchers have tried to augment the concept. The augmentations have often incorporated causal factors in an ad hoc fashion or through experimentation with existing data. These adaptations are similar to informal methods and usually lack a strong grounding in economic or other social science theory. Some have concluded that the predictive power of such approaches is questionable. Unfortunately, these critics have yet to offer alternatives that overcome the problems they raise. We believe that the approaches/models presented in this chapter are at least valuable as an aid to systematic and explicit thinking. Innovative application of the existing approaches may yield valid results in individual cases. If attempts at systematic market estimation are not made, the decision maker will be forced to return to gut feeling and intuition for his or her forecasts.

Despite the drawbacks and problems with innovation diffusion curves, they are one of the few analytic techniques available to the new venture analyst. The S-shaped substitution curve can be used to estimate company sales. Annual sales begin to grow slowly, even if market potential is large, and then continue at an increasing and later at a decreasing rate. Finally, after a period, sales asymptotically approach their potential. The resulting sales forecasts can then be used in other aspects of the new venture decision process.

6

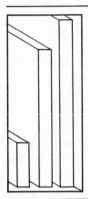

New Venture Analysis: Competitors

Introduction

Analyzing competitors forces new venture managers to focus on what aspects of their products are truly unique. It eliminates the comforting feeling that everything about the venture is new and different and focuses strategic thinking on that handful of features that no other product offers your customers.

Competitive analysis is comprised of a set of techniques that we use to modify the results of the market analysis. The outcome of the market analysis effort is a series of predictions of total annual company sales. Those predictions were based on the estimate of total market potential modified by the expected lags in consumer acceptance (see Chapter 5). Competitive analysis further reduces the sales prediction by accounting for the actions of other sellers over time. In this chapter, we will explore various ways to predict the actions of competitors and the resulting impacts on your venture's sales.

The idea of systematically examining competitors is relatively new to the field of business research. Although every company is concerned about competition, few organized techniques have been developed that add any useful insights to that concern. The state of the art is even less developed with respect to new ventures. Therefore, based on our experience and on the tools available in the business literature, we have organized an approach to competitor analysis in a new venture setting. We will begin by briefly reviewing two early attempts to deal with competition in a new venture analysis and then turn to a more recent approach formulated by Michael E. Porter (1980) at the Harvard Business School. Our approach to a more comprehensive treatment of this subject will also be explained. The chapter will close with an explanation of the practical problems of collecting data on competitors and with some suggestions for overcoming those problems.

Alternative Approaches to Competitor Analysis

Any company, whether a large existing firm or a small, start-up enterprise, is an extremely complex entity. Competitor analysis is based on the premise that the actions of a firm can be predicted by knowing only a few key facts about it. Two problems must be faced. The first is determining which facts are relevant and the second is interpreting what those facts mean. The approaches that have been developed to analyze competitors have made assumptions in an effort to overcome both of these problems. Those assumptions are sometimes based on empirical research, but often their only basis is common sense or intuition. Even those assumptions based on completed empirical research have shortcomings. The primary reason for these short-comings is that, as in any social science, it is not usually possible to conduct experiments on an ongoing corporation. The research is generally based on identified statistical correlations between a set of key facts that should be causally related to the firm's subsequent actions. It is often difficult but usually possible to measure these types of correlations. Measuring causality is much more difficult and cannot be done in the uncontrolled environment of the business world. Therefore, competitive analysis remains more of an art form than a science. In fact, we would argue that it is closer to a craft than an art.

We look for completeness of treatment as the key determinant of the value of various analytical approaches. That completeness must then be weighed against the difficulty and cost of actually using the approach in a new venture setting. We will begin our review of competitor analysis tools with the narrowest approach and successively incorporate more factors.

Perhaps the simplest way to treat competition in new venture analysis is to ask a question about the cost position of each firm relative to the whole industry. Wade Blackman included the question, Can the product be made as cheaply as competitors'? That is one of seven questions that Blackman uses in his preliminary new venture screening process (see review in Chapter 2). The question is preceded by the definition of market needs and products that fit those needs.

After internal manufacturing costs are estimated, the competitive question is addressed. If the question is answered no, the new venture idea is dropped. If the company can produce the product more inexpensively than its competitors, the screening process continues.

Blackman's approach is appealing in its simplicity. However, it suffers from numerous shortcomings. A variety of strategies other than cost leadership can lead to significant new venture profits. For example, consumers may be more interested in special features or unique ideas than in costs. Further, new ventures that can establish a proprietary position will earn significant returns without ever gaining cost leadership. In fact, our experience indicates that being the lowest cost producer is only one of many ways of being unique. For example, Tandem computers are unique because they are so reliable. The cost of redundant capability within the computer is significant, but the reliability is sometimes worth the price. Diablo letter-quality printers are not cost leaders, but their speed and durability in heavy workload environments make them valuable to consumers. Mercedes Benz automobiles have a reputation for high quality, luxury, and status appeal that clearly differentiate them from lower cost competitors. Thousands of similar examples could also be mentioned in which cost leadership is not the key to sales growth.

Venture capitalists spend a considerable amount of time investigating what aspects of an entrepreneur's product are unique to the marketplace. It is not only difficult but extremely costly to use a strategy of lowest cost to begin a new venture. Even major companies with vast resources are not using this strategy to launch their new ventures. The IBM Personal Computer (PC) is not the lowest priced personal computer. IBM has been careful not to completely alienate its target market by charging a price that is too high relative to its competitors. The success of the venture is most strongly tied to recognition of the name IBM and the resulting consumer expectations of permanence, high quality, reliability, and service.

If a competitive strategy of cost leadership is to be pursued, it is usually based on unique attributes, design, or production approaches rather than pure economies of scale. Economies of scale refer to the phenomenon that low unit costs are a result of increasing the number of units produced. Learning curve effects (discussed in Chapter 7), increased efficiencies in procuring and handling materials, lower component prices based on larger orders, more cost-effective machinery, and better machine and worker utilization are all factors that can produce economies of scale in manufacturing. Economies of scale effects require time and significant investments to obtain. To the new venture, investments of the magnitude required are difficult to obtain and leave the venture exposed to changes in the market. However, if unique production processes or product designs result in lower costs, the venture may have a viable competitive strategy for gaining market share.

The Du Pont company takes a different approach to competitive analysis than Blackman. Du Pont examines the "marketing leadership" of a new venture rather than cost leadership. Their approach is built on the assumption that competitive pressures will reduce market share as the market grows. The Du Pont approach uses the competitor analysis to modify (reduce) the market analysis results. The key competitive issue they include is the amount of lead time that their product has before competitors enter. Lead time is the amount of time that your new product is in the market before competitive alternatives are available to consumers. During that period, the new venture is in the enviable position of capturing the total market and all its growth. In other words, total market growth is equivalent to the sales growth for the company, and the venture's market share is 100 percent. For example, when Otis Elevator Company built the first elevator, they had 100 percent world market share. They were then asked to build another elevator. The market had doubled and they still held 100 percent share. After a few more elevators were installed, another company finally built one, at which point Otis elevator's market share dropped and their lead time was over.

When competitive products are introduced, the customer is choosing among similar products rather than buying the new venture's unique services. Lead time is determined by the proprietary position of the firm (in the form of patents and trade secrets or other unpatented know-how), and by the activities of competitors (based on their current abilities and status). Du Pont's framework for lead time estimation is conceptually richer than Blackman's approach. Both require exceptional judgment to carry out. There is no simple mathematical relationship that allows lead time to be estimated. The actions of numerous potential competitors must be predicted and those actions are not always economically rational. Your new venture management team must use a considerable amount of judgment to make lead time estimates.

Once a competitor's product is introduced, lead time has expired. After that date, various competitors will be vying for market share. Factors such as cost leadership, service, name recognition, established distribution chains, direct selling, advertising, and the ongoing introduction of further innovations will determine the extent to which your new venture's market share will deteriorate.

The calculation of market share after other products have been introduced is the final step in Du Pont's competitive analysis. Likely competitors are identified, and the market share of each is predicted over time using whatever knowledge is available in the company. To estimate these market shares, Du Pont (1971) suggests the following six-step process:

1. Identify likely, in-kind competitors.
2. Assess the strengths, weaknesses, and incentives of each competitor.
3. Do (on paper) what each competitor should do to maximize the worth of the venture; assume that his or her actions will be rational.
4. Identify your response to their most likely actions.
5. Repeat steps 3 and 4 for subsequent interactions over the time period of interest.
6. Summarize (year by year) relative shares of market for all competitors.

After the relative shares of all competitors are added together (step 6 above), they are subtracted from 100 percent. The difference is your venture's market share per year.

The resources required to accomplish these six steps can be significant. Gathering enough information to assess the strengths and weaknesses of each competitor is the largest hurdle to overcome. The data needed to estimate strategic direction is the same as the data that most companies try to keep out of the public domain. We will return to the difficult issues of gathering and interpreting data later in the chapter. Before tackling that issue, let us review some more recent advances in competitor analysis.

One of the most important advances has been developed by Michael Porter at the Harvard Business School. His book (1980) provides a much richer approach than that of either Du Pont (1971) or Blackman (1972). Porter takes the insights gained from the economic specialty of industrial organization and applies them to business strategy. The richness of Porter's approach comes from the simultaneous treatment of competition within the industry, potential entrants, potential substitutes, buyers, and suppliers. Figure 6–1 shows how Porter relates these key competitive factors.

The figure demonstrates that Porter is concerned with business strategy in general and not just with new ventures. The key motivation for a company's actions is assumed to be gaining and maintaining higher than normal returns from the business. The latter can only be achieved and sustained if the company can prevent competitors, buyers, suppliers, substitutes, or new entrants from eroding its market power. The company's strategy, therefore, must be designed to achieve and maintain market power. This premise is analogous to the concept of creating and maintaining economic value and is thus useful in new

FIGURE 6-1
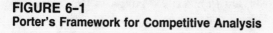
Porter's Framework for Competitive Analysis

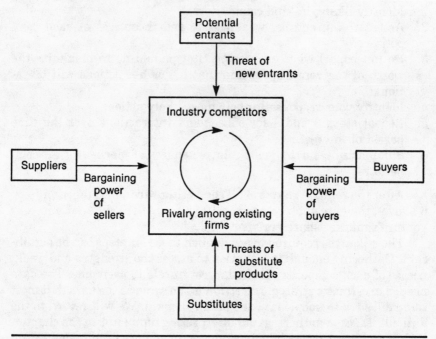

Source: Reprinted with permission of The Free Press, a Division of Macmillan Inc., from *Competitive Strategy: Techniques for Analyzing Industry and Competitors,* by Michael E. Porter. Copyright © 1980 by the Free Press.

venture analysis. Using this premise, Porter's framework allows the new venture analyst to systematically review all the factors that could dilute the economic value of the new venture.

A new venture usually requires entry into a new business. Porter identified situations that are most likely to allow an entering firm to create and maintain economic value. The first is an industry that is either just emerging or is undergoing rapidly changing conditions. Some new ventures are so unique that an identifiable market does not yet exist. With the introduction of the new venture's product, a market is created and an industry soon develops. The other industry situations identified by Porter (1980) where entry of a new venture's products can be attractive are:

1. Industries or sectors in which slow or ineffectual retaliation from incumbents may be expected.
2. Sectors where the new venture has lower entry costs than other

firms (often caused by some unique concept, technology, or production process).

3. Industries in which the firm has a distinctive ability to influence industry structure (for example, the entry of IBM into the personal computer market).

4. Industries where there will be positive effects on a firm's existing businesses resulting from the introduction of the new venture's products.

We have used Porter's framework as the basis for numerous competitor analyses. As you would expect, it is most useful when an established firm is examining its traditional businesses and competitors. The required data and insights are usually available or can be collected by surveying your firm's marketing department. Porter's framework provides a convenient place for everyone's insights and allows the analyst to draw strong conclusions about strategy. The framework also can be used to clearly demonstrate to management the logic behind the conclusions. Many of the same strengths can be applied to the anlaysis of competitors to a new venture.

Figure 6-2 presents an example of the use of Porter's competitive analysis framework in a new venture setting. In 1983, we assisted a company that was considering a new venture into the electronic warfare market in the United States. Electronic warfare refers to an array of technologies used by the military to assure that communications among friendly forces can be made without jamming or altering by the enemy, and to deny that privilege to the enemy.

The electronic warfare market is already established and a small number of prime U.S. government contractors (for example, E-Systems, Loral Corporation, Raytheon, Northrup, GTE-Sylvania) dominate that market. The figure shows that there is little threat to the market position of the established companies from substitute products or suppliers. The market is characterized by a single customer (the U.S. Department of Defense) who has the bulk of control over it. A new venture could successfully penetrate this market if it was able to develop a new and unique variation on current technology. If the Department of Defense recognized the value of the technology, the incumbent contractors could not prevent your market entry. Entry costs would include significant development expenses but relatively low marketing expenses.

We have often noticed that trying to complete the Porter framework graphically demonstrates how little a new venture's management knows about the industry it is about to enter. The development of new venture products is all too often an inwardly focused activity. It is driven by technical problems, scheduling problems, and personnel and

FIGURE 6-2
Example of Use of Porter's Framework for Competitor Analysis: U.S. Electronic Warfare Market

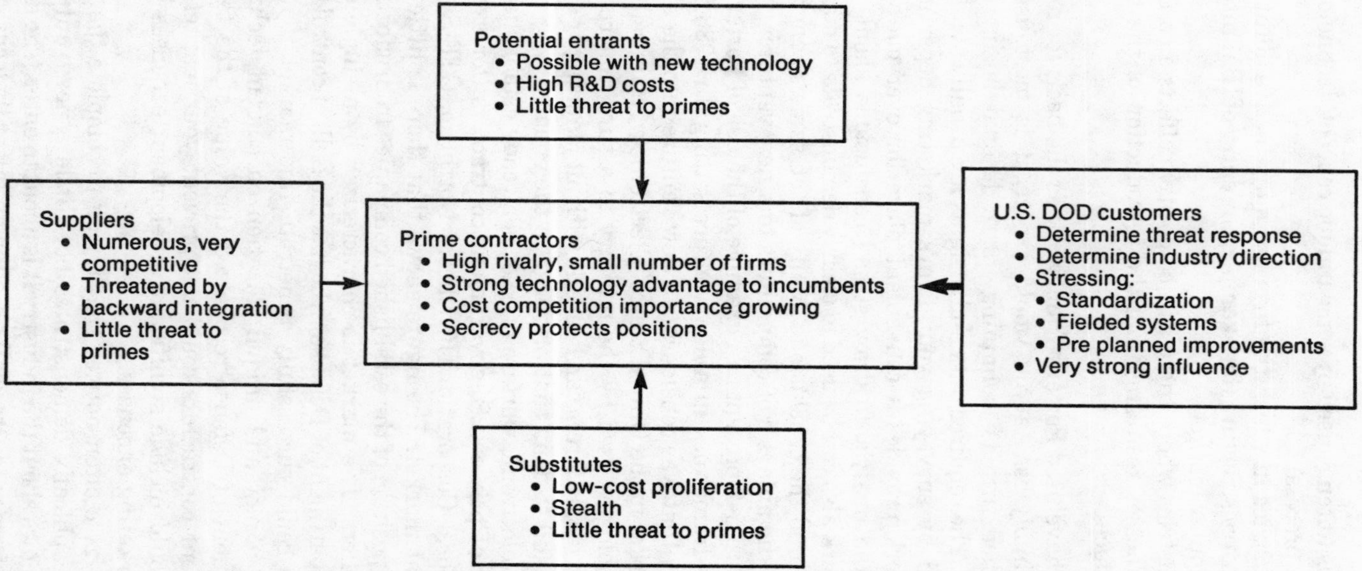

Potential entrants
- Possible with new technology
- High R&D costs
- Little threat to primes

U.S. DOD customers
- Determine threat response
- Determine industry direction
- Stressing:
  - Standardization
  - Fielded systems
  - Pre planned improvements
  - Very strong influence

Prime contractors
- High rivalry, small number of firms
- Strong technology advantage to incumbents
- Cost competition importance growing
- Secrecy protects positions

Suppliers
- Numerous, very competitive
- Threatened by backward integration
- Little threat to primes

Substitutes
- Low-cost proliferation
- Stealth
- Little threat to primes

planning problems. Even if it has had the benefits of continuing inputs from users (or potential users), only one element of the competitive industry has been explored. Many new ventures address markets not traditionally served by the venturing firm. Therefore, the rest of the company cannot provide much relevant competitive data.

We have incorporated many of the insights of Porter's framework into a more comprehensive competitor assessment approach. Figure 6–3 presents that approach. The right side of the figure shows the competitive analysis. If the industry is new and the venture represents the first offering (that is, it is not a copy of someone else's new venture), two calculations must be performed. First, the lead time has to be estimated. Key factors that determine lead time are listed in the figure. Entry costs are the first of these factors. These are the costs that another firm must bear in order to successfully enter your market. Some entry costs represent direct cash outlays to purchase production facilities, establish distribution channels, or conduct required product development. Other entry costs are more subtle. They can be manifest in the time delays required to develop ways around your patents, obtain needed regulatory approvals, or obtain the needed trade secrets of the business. For example, the time required to obtain regulatory approvals is particularly significant in the U.S. food and drug industries. Other factors crucial to an estimate of your venture's lead time are the interest of the senior management of your most likely competitor, the strategic importance of your market to competitors, and the general responsiveness of competitors to changing market conditions. The latter factor is usually reflected in the previous behavior of competitors in similar situations.

The second calculation for a new industry shown in the figure is the rate of market share erosion after competitors have entered your market. The figure lists six indicators of how quickly one can expect market share to erode. The six indicators are similar to the factors determining your product's lead time, but they are oriented toward the behavior of buyers rather than the motivations of competitors. The first two indicators address the attitudes of buyers toward new products in general and your product in particular. Markets such as oil and gas exploration services have traditionally been willing to accept innovative technologies if they could demonstrate a higher probability of discovering oil or gas. Innovations introduced in the home-building industry traditionally have not been quickly adopted. The reluctance of the industry to accept factory-built houses is one example.

The next key indicator of market share erosion is the extent to which your product is seen as different from those offered by competitors. The general reputation of competitors in the market also will influence market share erosion. The dramatic loss of market share in

FIGURE 6-3
Suggested Framework for Competitor Analysis of New Ventures

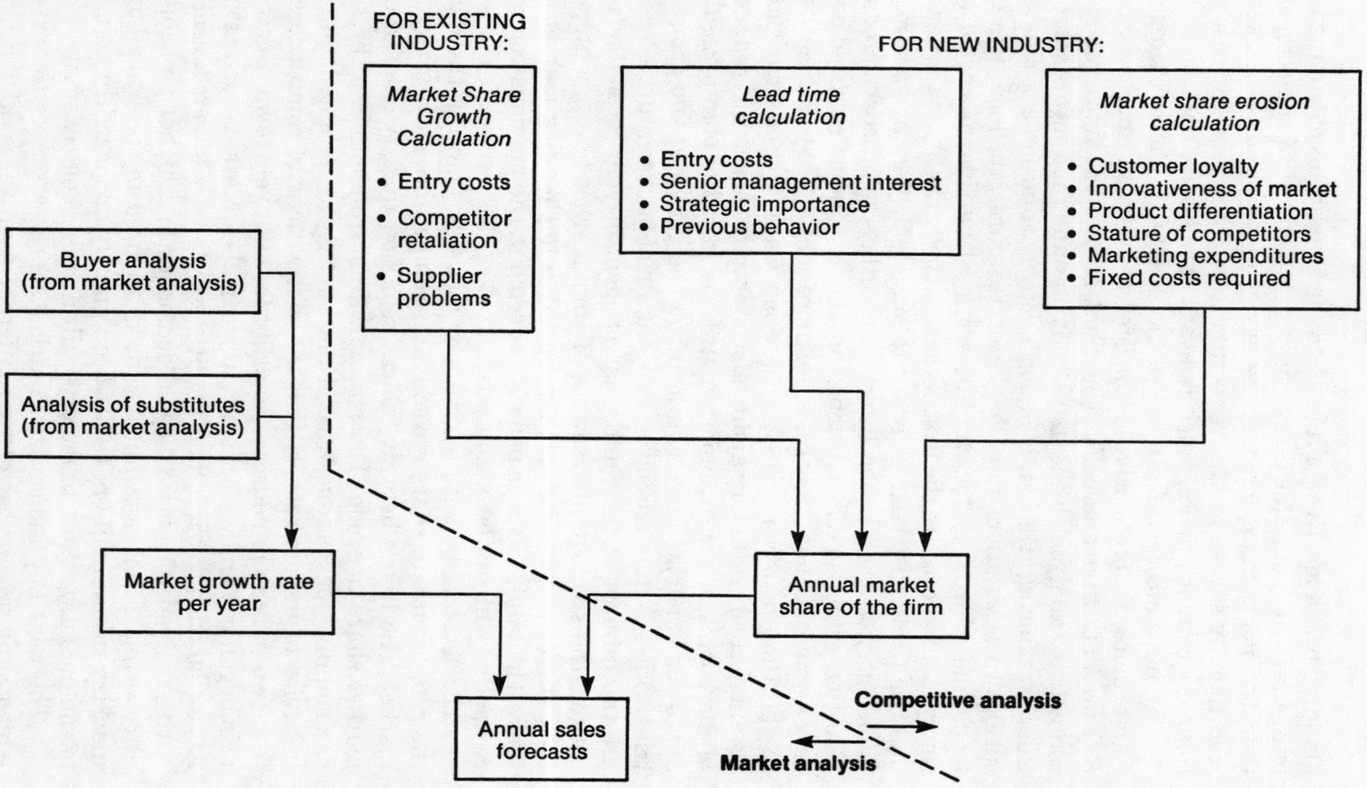

FOR NEW INDUSTRY:

Market share erosion calculation
• Customer loyalty
• Innovativeness of market
• Product differentiation
• Stature of competitors
• Marketing expenditures
• Fixed costs required

Lead time calculation
• Entry costs
• Senior management interest
• Strategic importance
• Previous behavior

FOR EXISTING INDUSTRY:

Market Share Growth Calculation
• Entry costs
• Competitor retaliation
• Supplier problems

Annual market share of the firm

Annual sales forecasts

Competitive analysis

Market analysis

Buyer analysis (from market analysis)

Analysis of substitutes (from market analysis)

Market growth rate per year

home computers experienced by the Apple Computer Company and some of the smaller home computer manufacturers was directly related to the stature of IBM in the eyes of customers. The final two indicators, fixed cost requirements and marketing expenditures, dictate how quickly competitors can expand their production and sales capacity to gain market share. For example, the fixed costs required to enter the commercial communications satellite market can total billions. The dominant commercial satellite producer, Hughes Aircraft Company, has not been a serious erosion of its market share, even with the entry of major competitors such as RCA or Ford Aerospace. Losing significant market share to other new ventures in the commercial satellite business is unlikely to occur quickly.

The upper middle portion of Figure 6-3 lists the types of analyses that would be done if the venture were to enter markets that were already well established. In these situations, the management of the venture must estimate market share growth over time rather than lead times and share erosion. The three factors most useful in estimating how to gain market share are your entry costs, expected retaliatory actions by existing producers, and the capabilities and priorities of your suppliers.

The remainder of the figure illustrates how the competitive information and analysis is used to modify your annual sales forecast. The result of the competitor evaluation is a prediction of your venture's annual market share (as a percent of total market). The market analyses discussed in Chapter 5 resulted in an estimate of total sales each year without regarding competitive pressures. Those market share estimates should be used to reduce the original results of the market analysis in order to acquire more accurate annual sales forecasts.

The approach outlined in Figure 6-3 is oriented toward judgment rather than numerical manipulation. Given the additional uncertainties surrounding the new venture, this level of treatment is appropriate. Consideration of competition from the perspective of the whole industry yields most of the insights needed at this point in the new venture decision process.

We have not yet discussed what is probably the most detailed competitor analysis framework. The approach involves the use of more traditional strategic planning techniques applied to competitors, some of which will be reviewed in Chapter 10. When used in a competitor analysis, these techniques allow the analyst to predict a competitor's behavior by simulating his or her entire strategic planning process. This can be an exhaustive process. Furthermore, the extra effort does not usually yield superior results since a relatively small amount of data is overworked by the analytical tools. The sophistication and depth of available data are not commensurate with the demands placed upon it. The new venture faces so many other problems that it is best to keep the competitor analysis fairly simple.

Data Collection and Interpretation

The ideal pieces of information needed to understand your competitors would be a summary of each of their strategic plans and a sample of the products they will be introducing in the future. This information is, of course, some of the most closely guarded by any company. However, keeping the idea in mind is useful as it serves as a reminder to focus the practical search for data on the most relevant facts.

The first piece of practical data needed is the names of the most likely competitors. If your venture will enter a well-established market, competitors may be well known. If it opens a new market, identification of competitors can be one of the most difficult aspects of the analysis. Part of the difficulty stems from the variety of forms that competitors can take. At least some of your competitors probably will be new start-ups backed by venture capitalists. The principals of the start-ups could easily have been your key employees. Other competitors may be small- to medium-sized firms that currently produce related products or serve your potential customers in another capacity. Competitors of this type can usually be identified after a market study. Your competitors may also be a division or smaller operating unit of a diversified firm. The difficulty here is that relevant information is usually not available for small units of larger companies. Finally, competitors may be new ventures of medium- or large-sized firms. In this situation, there may be little or no knowledge of these ventures within the target markets. Information on such ventures will be even more difficult to obtain here than in the other forms that competitors may take.

The organizational form a competitor takes compounds the difficulty in collecting information about him or her. The type of information needed does not vary across competitors. Practical information which is both useful and possible to obtain on each major competitor includes:

1. General Goals and Objectives.   These are often stated in annual reports to stockholders, speeches, or other public statements made by senior management or included in business periodical articles about the company (for example, *The Wall Street Journal, Business Week, Barron's, Venture*). Brochures and other promotional material produced by competitors may also be useful.

2. Financial Data. Sales, net income, current assets, and investments in plant and equipment can provide insight into a competitor's financial management abilities and available resources. Securities and Exchange Commission (SEC) filings are required for publically traded companies and are available to the public. The most widely used report is called the "10–K" report. 10–K reports provide a great deal of financial and management detail about the firm and are usually quite helpful. Financial data on start-up companies, closely held companies, or new ventures within larger companies are not generally available. Sometimes it is possible to obtain some basic sales and income data from research departments at investment banks or brokerage firms, or by simply calling the company.

3. Facilities. Some descriptions of physical plant and equipment are included in 10–K reports and in annual reports. More detailed information about specific equipment and/or the extent of its manufacturing capabilities can sometimes be obtained by reviewing articles in local newspapers where the facilities are located.

4. Technological and Strategic Thrusts. We have found business periodical articles and articles in specialized trade magazines to be the most useful sources of this data. We usually begin with a computer-based search of the business literature to find citations and/or abstracts of recent articles. Many local libraries offer these types of searches at a reasonable cost. The same computer-based search procedure can be used to recreate a history of the company's products and market strategies over the past three to five years. Competitors' brochures or company newspapers may provide additional insights.

5. Market Perceptions and Relative Market Position. Market studies prepared by investment banks, stock brokerage firms, or consulting firms are useful if they can be located. Firms such as Frost and Sullivan, Inc., Arthur D. Little, Inc., and SRI International, Inc. conduct a large number of detailed market studies that are available for sale. Smaller consulting firms specializing in one or two markets are another good source of market position data on competitors. If none of these approaches prove useful, the new venture can conduct an informal market survey using the telephone. If it is well planned, the survey can be used in both the market research (Chapter 5) and competitor analysis.

6. Overall Strengths and Weaknesses. Some effort should be made to summarize the competitive analysis conducted on each company. A convenient format for the summary is to list major strengths and weaknesses of each company.

For example, major strengths may include statements such as:

The competitor tends to offer innovative financing packages along with its products to attract major customers.

New ventures launched by the company tend to receive the benefit of production facilities shared with existing product lines.

The new venture will be allowed to use the parent's existing retail distribution chain.

The parent company's image of high quality services will yield benefits to the new venture in its target market sector.

Examples of overall weaknesses of the new venture may be:

New venture production costs will be high because the parent company specializes in development and one-of-a-kind fabrication rather than mass production.

The new venture's target market is not understood by the parent company.

The new venture will require a large amount of resources relative to the size of the parent company.

The parent company is accustomed to higher profit margins and higher overhead costs than will be tolerated in the new venture's target market.

The parent company is not accustomed to constant product development efforts needed to keep pace with competitors in the target market.

The data sources explained above are generally available to the public and can be obtained at reasonable costs. There is another, perhaps more useful, source of information: personal contacts. An amazing amount of information can be gathered by using the telephone. Begin the process with the names of a few acquaintances. We have found that most people are willing to discuss other companies and usually know the names of people who know more about specific issues. Sociologists term this approach *networking*. The types of people with the best information about competitors include investment bankers specializing in the industry, suppliers (both to you and your competitors), technical and market consultants in related industries, key customers, trade association members, and journalists serving related industries. Attendance at trade shows and conferences is a natural extension of the personal contact approach to data gathering.

Summary

Analyzing competitors can be frustrating and time consuming. The data obtained are often incomplete and irrelevant. The approaches used to translate the data into useful conclusions are incomplete and require extensive use of judgment by the analyst. Given these facts, the value of conducting competitor analysis in a new venture setting can be questioned. New venture managers face a myriad of demands on their time and resources. It is relatively easy to decide to completely forgo any organized competitor analysis or to spend only a minimal amount of time on the effort.

The success of a new venture is better served by withstanding some unpleasantness and incurring the costs necessary to conduct a more thorough investigation of competitors. The insights provided by the investigation can help make the difference between a set of "interesting" results and a practical new venture plan with a high probability of success. We are not advocating an exhaustive effort on competitor analysis. As mentioned earlier, attempts to recreate a competitor's entire strategic planning process are not, in most cases, justified.

The competitor analysis in a new venture setting cannot be conducted only once. There is a need for an ongoing investigation that grows in complexity with the growth of the venture's sales and the maturation of its markets. Competitor analysis should remain an integral element of the strategic planning of the venture through its entire life. There are at least four reasons for supporting an ongoing effort. First, it takes time to gather information and to gain the experience necessary to interpret the data in a meaningful way. Second, the quality of the analysis also improves with management reviews and further iterations of the process. Third, the new venture environment is dynamic. Competitor strategies and products continuously change. Monitoring competitors activities over time provides insights into attitudes and tendencies that are difficult to obtain by reviewing historical documents. Fourth, your network of personal contacts will expand and become useful over time.

Competitor analysis is a craft that yields better results as both the analyst and the new venture management team gain experience with it.

7

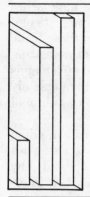

New Venture Analysis: Costs

Introduction

The third type of inquiry done in a new venture analysis is an examination of costs. The management team must predict both the nonrecurring costs of the venture (research and development costs plus capital equipment and facilities costs) and the recurring costs associated with different levels of production. The latter costs include (1) raw materials, (2) production labor costs, (3) selling expenses, and (4) general and administrative costs. If the new venture provides a service rather than a product, there will be a slightly different set of recurring costs.

Cost analysis is usually the most straightforward and therefore the easiest part of a venture analysis. Costs are largely under the direct control of the firm. Many engineers and production specialists have considerable knowledge of the cost characteristics of the firm's current products. Most firms have resident staffs of experts who are well versed in the details of cost estimating. Although the new venture is, by definition, a first-time product, process, or service for the firm, some of the production steps may be quite similar to those taken for existing products. To the extent possible, standard cost estimation techniques should be used.

We have seen cases where the existing cost estimation methodologies are biased against new ventures. For example, if the firm's traditional products do not exhibit cost reductions with volume increases, the costing methodology may ignore such cost dynamics. If that firm is considering a new venture in which costs are driven by production volume, the venture's management is faced with an additional challenge: The cost estimation department must either modify its methodology for this venture, or the venture's management must estimate costs without the aid of this department. Either route is difficult. The new venture's managers must convince senior management that the cost estimates are credible even though they are at variance with the firm's traditional cost estimation practice.

The analyst estimating costs of a new venture must gather the relevant information and transpose it into a usable form. The cost information has to capture the incremental impact of the venture on the firm's cash flow position over time. Therefore, the information may take a form considerably different from detailed accounting results. For example, the marginal impact of the new venture on the firm's tax liability is relevant to the venture analysis but is probably not relevant to the cost estimating department of the division where the venture resides. In most cases, the new venture analyst must take a broader view of costs than is typically done at the cost or profit center level. He or she must review all costs from the viewpoint of the entire corporation and should act as if s/he is the chief financial officer of a separate corporation conducting the venture. Further, s/he must be extremely careful to only include the incremental costs of the new venture on the parent firm. It is not correct to add the new venture product to the existing manufacturing base and then calculate new average costs for all the products. The relevant cost is the difference between the total production costs before the new venture and the total costs after the product is incorporated into the production flow.

This chapter focuses on the estimation of the recurring costs of a new venture. R&D and capital equipment costs have to be considered separately from recurring costs. Estimates of these costs are based on preliminary engineering designs and the expertise of cost engineers. They are crucial to a venture analysis but they are estimated earlier in the process than recurring costs. The R&D and capital equipment costs do not demonstrate the dynamic changes that can occur in production (that is, recurring) costs. The nonrecurring costs can be subject to large uncertainties and long debates. There are few tools available to help the analyst with the estimates. It is best to conduct a detailed cost estimate from the lowest possible level of aggregation (that is, from the bottom up), and to document all the assumptions of the estimate. Rules of thumb or other shortcuts to estimating nonrecurring costs usually do not survive reviews by senior management or skeptical cost auditors. The analyst is then forced to reestimate costs based on a detailed, bottom up exercise. We believe it is more efficient to spend more time early to do the extended cost estimate, and to generate the rationale to defend that estimate later in the new venture decision process.

Let us turn to the recurring production costs of the new venture. If recurring costs are expected to remain stable over time or merely increase with inflation, they should be estimated in a manner similar to the nonrecurring costs. If they are expected to fluctuate over time, the analyst has a much different problem. Most estimations of the second type are based on the concepts of learning and experience curves. The objective of this chapter is to review what those concepts are, how they are used, and how reliable they are. The chapter will demonstrate the uncertainty that is buried in the estimation of future recurring costs.

The concepts of learning and experience, the limitations and potential pitfalls of those concepts, and a sample of the application of the concepts to a venture analysis are the subjects of this chapter.

Review of Learning and Experience Curve Concepts

Like many plausible notions, the learning curve concept was first offered as an explanation of an observed and persistent phenomenon. In the 1920s, businesspeople began to notice distinct relationships between production volume and unit costs in the production of airplanes. Their studies showed that with each doubling in the cumulative production of aircraft of a given type the number of worker-hours required declined to 80 percent of its previous level (Hirschmann, 1964). Furthermore, the 80 percent factor was found to be common to fighter bomber and transport planes. As a result, researchers began to hypothesize that a general theory or concept of learning existed. The core of the theory was that people learn by doing and that repetition of a given process leads its practitioners ever closer to "best practice," which can be defined as the maximum attainable efficiency consistent with the physical and economic limits governing the production process. In this restricted definition, "learning" occurs within a fixed production process and is ultimately bounded by some technical or economic limit. This convergence toward best practice has been termed the *learning curve*. The parameter most commonly used to describe learning curves is the "learning slope," the ratio of unit cost after a doubling of cumulative output to unit cost before the doubling.

In writing about learning curves, different authors have presented a wide variety of definitions of what changes are included in the phenomenon. A few examples illustrate the amount of confusion that surrounds the definition of learning curves. David L. Bodde defined learning curves to include changes in production methods, administrative organization, and in the product itself (Bodde, 1976). Martin Wolf, in an article written in the same year, included all technology development, including breakthroughs, automation, and complete changes in the production process in his definition (Wolf and Greenberg, 1976). Finally, Werner Hirsch defines the learning curve as follows: "The function is related to a number of points on different production functions involving successive changes in technical knowledge in a given facility" (Hirsch, 1952, p. 148).

One of the key articles on learning curves appeared in the *Harvard Business Review* in 1964. The article's author, W. B. Hirschmann, examined learning curves associated with various production inputs and phases of the production process. His analysis was also based on the airplane production industry. The importance of Hirschmann's article was not in how it defined learning curves. Rather, it gave some guidelines for applying learning curves to various production settings. Hirschmann concluded that in labor intensive production processes (that is, a three to one labor to machine input ratio), an 80 percent learning curve is common. If the ratio of labor and machine inputs is approximately one to one, the process usually shows an 85 percent learning curve slope. If the ratio of labor to machine inputs is one to three, the curve shows a slope of about 90 percent. Table 7–1 summarizes the learning curve examples cited by Hirschmann. The examples used range from learning in a single process within a plant (for example, GE plant maintenance record) to an entire industry (for example, the U.S. basic steel industry). The data cover various time periods from 1888 to 1969. The factors Hirschmann cites as contributing to the cost declines include both economies of scale and the impacts of R&D. In other words, even the slopes of learning curves used will depend on what is included in the definition. The learning curve slopes estimated by Hirschmann have stood the test of time and remain good guidelines for new venture cost estimation.

In 1968, the Boston Consulting Group (BCG) published a widely referenced book that drew a distinction between learning curves and experience curves. They defined experience curves in terms of the relationship between cumulative production and all costs incurred by the firm, including R&D, capital, overhead, labor, and materials. They also stated that the relationship can be applied to a single firm or to an entire industry. The authors made an important distinction between unit production costs and unit selling prices. If costs decline more rapidly than prices, competitors are stimulated to enter the market to capture some of the lucrative profits. Although the BCG contends that these differences are eventually eliminated, unstable market condi-

TABLE 7-1
Learning Curve Examples Presented by W. B. Hirschmann

Process or industry	Factors cited as influencing learning curve	Learning curve slope (constant dollars)	Data comments
Individual fluid catalytic cracking unit (one step in petroleum refining process)	Machine-dominated operation Learning by operators to extend output over rated capacity by reducing safety margins	90%	Data in late 1950s Single unit examined
General Electric plant maintenance record (average time per replacement of parts compared to cumulative number of replacements)	Labor-dominated operation Very repetitive nature of parts replacement process	76	1949–1956 Single plant
Construction of fluid catalytic cracking units	Construction is labor intensive Decline caused mainly by research and development improvements affecting plant design and technology improvements Economies of scale contributed to decline	80	1942–1958 Cost per unit constructed in 1942 compared to 1958 only
Labor-hour requirements in U.S. crude oil refining	Joint effort of learning in all companies and processes	85	1888–1962 Industrywide data
U.S. electric power industry, dollars/kw of capacity compared to millions of kw	Cumulative effect of learning in all companies and processes	75–80	1910–1955 Industrywide data
U.S. basic steel industry (labor-hours per unit output)	Cumulative effect of learning in all companies and processes	70–75	1920–1955 Industrywide data
Production of Ford Model T	Assembly is labor intensive	86	1910–1926 Price (not cost) per unit compared in 1910 and 1926

Source: W. B. Hirschmann, "Profit from the Learning Curve," 42, no. 1 (January, February 1964), pp. 127, 130, 131.

tions, caused by significant differences between unit costs and unit prices, can persist for long periods of time. The relationship between production volume and unit prices is therefore admitted by the authors to be less stable than the relationship between production volume and unit costs.

The BCG study presents experience curves for 24 products. Time periods vary in length and date from 1929 to 1968. The examples relate only the cumulative, industrywide production to the price per unit of output for the product. Due to the limited availability of data, cost per unit of output was not estimated. Table 7-2 summarizes the BCG examples. The majority of the examples show a significant change or kink in their experience curves. Prices of the products (in constant dollars) sometimes increased for short periods (for example, crude oil, 1946-1948; motor gasoline, 1946-1949; facial tissue, 1945-1948) and sometimes fluctuated up and down significantly (for example, primary aluminum, 1948-1963). Often prices remained constant with increased production (for example, ethylene, 1953-1963; titanium sponge, 1950-1954; and freestanding gas ranges, 1946-1950). Experience curve slopes between 70 and 90 percent dominated the sample. Almost all products with a kink in their experience curves showed the rate of price decline accelerating after the slope change. Slopes frequently changed from 90 to 70 percent or less. BCG explains this phenomenon as the result of the dominant firm allowing prices to decline less rapidly than costs, leading to increased profits that entice other companies to enter the market. To keep its relative market share, the dominant firm then allows prices to decline quickly, until they are decreasing at a rate equal to cost. Although it is an interesting explanation, this hypothesis was not tested in the BCG study.

Limitations to the Use of Learning and Experience Curves

There are many limitations to learning and experience curves. In fact, some have argued that experience curves lack any causal underpinnings and are of no value in predicting future costs. However, venture analysis is a heuristic approach to a set of very difficult practical problems. These practical considerations often override problems of theoretical limitations. We believe the most relevant perspective from which to view the concepts of learning and experience is one that investigates their practical usefulness. From that perspective, it is clear that the curves are useful and can be an important part of a venture analysis. However, the limitations have to be kept in mind.

The first practical limitation to the use of learning and experience

TABLE 7-2
Experience Curves Identified by the Boston Consulting Group
(cumulative industry production versus price)

Process or industry	Learning curve slope (constant dollars)		Data comments
Germanium transistors industry	90%	(1954–1960)	1954–1968
	70	(1960–1968)	
Silicon transistors industry	90	(1954–1959)	
			1954–1969
	70	(1960–1965)	
	80	(1965–1969)	
Germanium diodes	90	(1955–1960)	1955–1968
	70	(1960–1968)	
Silicon diodes	90	(1955–1959)	1955–1968
	70	(1960–1968)	
Integrated circuits	70		1964–1968 (1965 and 1966 monthly data)
Crude oil (prices increased 1946–1948)			1946–1968 Real prices increased from 1946–1948
	90	(1948–1958)	
	70	(1958–1968)	
Motor gasoline (prices increased (1946–1949)			1946–1968 (average price/gallon excluding California)
	90	(1949–1957)	
	75	(1957–1968)	U.S. data only
Ethylene	100	(1953–1963)	1953–1968
	70	(1963–1968)	U.S. tariff price versus U.S. data only
Benzene	70	(1953–1963)	1952–1968
	90	(1963–1968)	U.S. data only
Paraxylene	90	(1957–1961)	1957–1968
	70	(1961–1968)	
Low-density polyethylene	90	(1952–1959)	1952–1968
	70	(1960–1968)	
Polypropylene	90	(1959–1961)	1959–1968
	80	(1961–1968)	
Polystyrene (general purpose molding and extrusion resin)	90	(1943–1954)	1943–1968
	70	(1954–1968)	
Polyvinylchloride	90	(1946–1955)	1946–1968
	70	(1955–1961)	
	80	(1961–1968)	
Primary aluminum	80	(1929–1939)	1929–1968
	70	(1939–1948)	
	no trend	(1948–1968)	
Primary magnesium	80–90		1929–1968 Significant deviations in trend

TABLE 7-2 (*concluded*)

Process or industry	Learning curve slope (constant dollars)		Data comments
Titanium sponge	100	(1950–1954)	1950–1968
	70	(1954–1968)	Strong deviation between 1958–1968
Monochrome television receivers	90	(1947–1954)	1947–1968
	70	(1954–1968)	
Total freestanding gas ranges	100	(1946–1950)	1946–1967
	70	(1950–1967)	Average wholesale prices
Total freestanding electric ranges	90	(1946–1957)	1946–1967
	70	(1957–1967)	
Facial tissue	90	(1933–1945)	1933–1966
	increases	(1945–1948)	
	90	(1948–1966)	
Japanese beer	80–90		1951–1968 Retail price minus indirect tax
Electric power	70	(1939–1943)	1939–1968
	80	(1943–1968)	
Refined cane sugar	70		1935–1968, Very wide fluctuations in data

Source: Boston Consulting Group, Inc., *Perspectives on Experience* (Boston: Boston Consulting Group, 1968), pp. 30–94.

curves in a venture analysis is the lack of any generally agreeable definition of either concept. We saw that a number of alternative definitions appeared in the business literature. Very few of these definitions differentiate (1) movements along a single learning curve, (2) shifts in the learning curve, and (3) the factors included in the concept of an experience curve. We have found the following definitions adequate to solve this problem in a manner that allows different parts of the same organization to more easily communicate.

The definition of a learning curve can be restricted to the relationship between cumulative production and the direct unit costs of a single input (for example, labor). It is a measure of improved performance within one particular production process. A changeover to a new production process is then considered a shift in the learning curve.

Changes in the variable inputs to the production process (variable inputs are those factors of production whose cost varies with short-term fluctuations in output) create a movement along the learning curve. Any changes in the fixed inputs to the production process (fixed inputs are those factors of production whose level of use does not vary with short-term fluctuations in output) are defined as a switch in processes and, hence, a shift in the learning curve. In other words, improvements in the efficiency or organization of the work force, management, or any other single variable input are regarded as movements along the learning curve. Changes in production scale or changes in the technology embodied in the fixed capital, on the other hand, are considered shifts in the learning curve.

These more precise definitions will enable a firm to separate those forces causing shifts in the learning curve from those causing movements along the curve, a vital distinction with respect to cost predictions for a new venture.

Experience curves can then be defined as the relationship between cumulative production and all production costs (including indirect costs such as development costs, retooling costs, and marketing). Therefore, the experience curve for a particular company or industry is determined by the learning curves for each production process (and input) plus the effects on cost of indirect outlays incurred by the company.

Clear and mutually agreeable definitions of these three aspects of cost reduction will help avoid some of the other limitations in the application of learning and experience concepts.

A second problem in using the concepts of learning and experience concerns the level of aggregation to which they should be applied. Most products are not made in a single process or even at a single location. Cost reductions of a product are comprised of distinct learning effects of the components that make up that product. Unfortunately, many applications of the learning concept are conducted at the product rather than the component level. It is ironic that this limitation to the learning concept was identified soon after the concept was formalized. In 1956, Harold Asher noticed the problem while also investigating airplane production learning effects. The production of airplanes is not a single process, but a collection of processes. Each of the processes is subject to its own learning curve. The learning curve of the final product is the sum of the individual process learning curves. It is unlikely that the final product's learning curve will show a simple percentage relationship to cumulative production. It will probably have kinks or flatten out with higher production volumes, or show some other complex relationship to volume. Asher found that if one assumed that the total airplane has a single, simple learning curve, errors were introduced in the cost estimation. The errors increased with output and were significant when output in that industry exceeded 300 units.

One could argue that even learning curves for components do not have a simple proportional relationship to volume. Asher was sufficiently thorough to examine this possibility. He concluded that the error introduced by this assumption is negligible. The best approach to learning curve modeling is to formulate the first unit costs and slopes of the key individual component learning curves, and then sum them to obtain the estimate of the entire product's learning curve. This approach allows all the existing knowledge about the component processes to be included in the estimate of the product's aggregate learning curve.

A third area of debate among learning curve experts is the range of output over which the proportional cost reduction phenomenon will continue. Many feel that the learning curve effect will continue for the entire lifetime of the product; others believe that there is a limit to the learning curve effect. In the view of the latter group, as the production process becomes more efficient, the cost can approach, but not reach, the cost of the raw materials. This cost imposes a lower bound on learning impacts. As the cost of the product approaches that of its raw materials, the learning curve will begin to level off. Reductions in unit cost beyond this limit can only be obtained by changing the types of raw materials used or changing the production technology. In other words, cost will only decline further by shifting the learning curve.

A closely related learning curve problem surrounds the question of measuring learning or experience from the correct starting point. A good example of this problem can be drawn from the field of renewable energy technologies. Photovoltaics is a type of solar energy conversion device that utilizes semiconductor technology to convert sunlight directly to electricity. The costs of the technology are extremely high, but most experts foresee significant experience curve effects leading to lower prices. The key question is what cost experience is relevant to the technology. If you view photovoltaics as a new generation silicon semiconductor device, the relevant cumulative production which has already occurred is massive. As a result, little cost reduction can be anticipated until sales of photovoltaics become very large. Alternatively, if you view photovoltaics as a new and unique device, substantial cost reduction will occur with relatively minor increases in production volume. It may be many years before we can clearly state which view is correct. Recently, however, the cost declines in the technology have slowed and the earlier projections are proving to be too optimistic. The price reductions have stalled, in part because demand for the technology has not expanded and in part because earlier learning curve effects were overestimated.

Misestimation of past, relevant, cumulative production can lead to serious errors in cost estimation. The tendency in most companies is to underestimate the relevant past experience and therefore over-estimate the expected declines in future costs. The decision about the experience or learning curve starting point is never obvious. Experts and managers within the company can have vastly different opinions, even if they share the goal of conducting a completely objective analysis.

Other key problems to be faced include:

1. Confusion by analysts about the role of time in the learning and experience curve concepts. The curves are based on the relationship between cumulative production and unit costs or prices. Time does not explain the reduction in cost. The confusion occurs because increases in cumulative production are often strongly correlated with time.

2. The product or components under study may be subject to cost declines due to experience shared with other products. Measuring the impact of shared experience on product cost trends is difficult. It is closely related to the problem of determining the correct starting point for the learning curve.

3. An often overlooked problem is the lack of available cost data. A firm may have watched numerous products proceed down a learning curve. However, slope estimates may not be available because data were not collected in a usable form. This reduces the analysis to a "best guess" approximation when much better information could have been obtained.

4. The slopes and starting points of experience curves facing competing firms may be quite different than those facing your firm. This can create problems in forecasting competitive responses.

Applications of Learning and Experience Curves to New Venture Analysis

Limitations to the application of learning and experience curves present many potential pitfalls to the new venture analyst. Nonetheless, the concepts are among the very few organized approaches that help predict future costs. We will review two examples of the application of learning and experience curves in new venture cost analysis. The first, developed at Du Pont, is primarily a prescription for conducting a new venture cost analysis on a commodity-oriented product. It provides a great deal of useful information on the mechanics of the analysis, but falls short of recommending how to avoid some of the more difficult pitfalls of using the curves. We developed the second example to demonstrate how to apply the concepts to a technology-oriented new venture.

Cost Analysis in a Commodity-Oriented New Venture

Cost analysis is a commodity-oriented new venture should begin by estimating capital and other nonrecurring costs. Material handling and processing equipment, production facilities, buildings, and storage requirements must be included in such an estimate. Recurring costs are divided into four separate cost areas: (1) raw materials, (2) conversion costs, (3) selling expenses, and (4) administrative costs. These four cost areas are later aggregated to determine the annual recurring cost for any given level of sales volume. The sales volume estimates should be the result of the market analysis conducted in Chapter 5.

When dealing with a commodity-related new venture, it is possible to put all cost estimates in a standard denomination (for example, pounds per year). This convention allows easy addition or other manipulation within the four cost divisions. Let us examine each cost area separately.

The raw material cost area includes all materials and energy entering the production cycle. It estimates the cost incurred based on the given sales volume estimate. The following should be included: (1) yields of raw material conversion, (2) uncertainties concerning how much material is actually needed to produce a unit (or pound) of the final product, and (3) raw material prices that vary with order quantities.

The conversion cost area includes estimates of all the remaining direct costs of manufacturing the product. These costs include direct manufacturing labor, power and services, depreciation of production equipment, maintenance labor and materials, pollution control, and any ongoing research support required.

Selling expenses include the following elements of selling costs: advertising, direct salesperson support, technical services support, and other marketing expenses. Selling expenses also include the freight costs of the product.

Administrative costs are grouped into (1) pioneering research, (2) general management expenses, and (3) all other expenses. These costs are predicted as dollars spent per year based on the annual unit sales volume assumption.

Cost Analysis in a Technology-Oriented New Venture

Price reduction is key to the successful commercial development of many new computer-based and energy technologies. One of our recent studies on renewable energy technologies relied on experience curves to forecast prices. The cost and price of the technology were estimated by separating the system into three major components: the collection subsystem, the balance of the energy conversion subsystem, and the integration of the system (assembly, installation, and expected profit margins). Each major component of the system was modeled separately with a unique set of experience curves. The three separate models were then summed to estimate the total price.

The energy collection subsystem was modeled by relating 1975 costs (excluding inflation) of the components to cumulative industry production. The initial cost was the current cost of those collection devices (in 1978), and the initial volume was an estimate of cumulative production between 1975 and 1978.

The decision to use only the energy collection devices as the basis for learning was rooted in an implicit assumption that those devices differ enough from similar, semiconductor devices to demonstrate a separate experience effect. To limit the impact of this implicit assumption, several features were added to the model. First, Figure 7–1 shows that each curve used in the model included a lower bound or minimum

FIGURE 7-1
Simplified Relationship between Cost and Production for Technology-Oriented New Venture

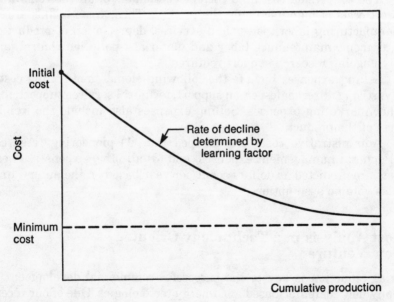

cost. The minimum cost approximated the cost of materials. In the case of the energy collection devices, it is expected that the production technology and the types of raw materials used will change over time. To represent this expected change, a second experience curve was introduced at the time the new technology might be introduced. The minimum cost and even the slope of the relevant experience curve would change at that time. Figure 7–2 graphically depicts the change. The two curves are labeled experience factors 1 and 2, respectively, in the figure. Cost declines followed the slope of experience curve 1 for the first stages in the product's life cycle. When the new technology was introduced, cost reductions then followed the slope of experience curve 2. The curves worked well in our study and we recommend this approach whenever a clear technology shift is likely in your new venture.

We also recognized that cost and price reduction will only occur under a relatively orderly market. If demand rises sharply and the industry has to increase production rapidly, there is little time or motivation for cost or price reduction (that is, a seller's market develops). Inefficiencies in running second and third shifts and other ex-

FIGURE 7-2
Price Reduction Formulation due to Technology Change in Technology-Oriented New Venture

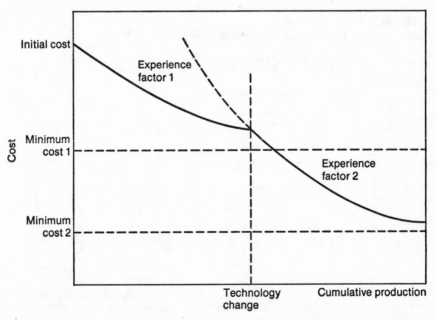

traordinary steps are taken to meet demand. The model developed in our study included a factor to represent the disruption in orderly cost reduction that occurs when there are major increases in demand. The factor used represents the fraction of manufactured units on which experience is gained in the year. Figure 7–3 shows the relationship we used. If production in the current year is twice as great as last year, no cost reduction from experience is realized in the year. If the ratio of production in this year to last year is 1.5, one half of the units produced in this year are applicable to the experience-induced annual cost reduction. The cost disruption factors we used may be considered severe in some new ventures. The values we used are only examples; any other volume/cost relationships can be easily applied to the approach.

The next major element of the system cost, the balance of system components, also used experience curves with lower cost bounds. This component was unique in that it included a shared experience factor. The energy collection devices can be combined with a variety of other components to make numerous types of systems serving different energy needs. For example, systems built to provide 175-watt outdoor lighting should share a great deal of experience with 250-watt outdoor lighting systems. However, building 175-watt outdoor lighting systems may yield little relevant experience for constructing gas pipeline

FIGURE 7–3
Operational Form of an Experience Disruption Model

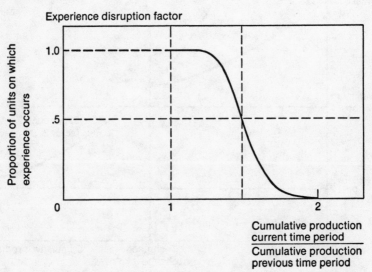

corrosion protection systems. Our study developed a matrix of all applications of the energy system and then estimated the degree of shared experience (as a percent) between all paired combinations.

If the products being produced in the new venture are not closely related, do not bother with shared experience effects. If there are only a few products produced and they are very closely related, it is easier to use a single experience curve for the entire product group. We have found that the best approach is to quiz the key technical or production personnel. If they believe shared production is going to be a cost driver, then explicitly model the phenomenon.

The final component of our example is system integration. We defined integration to include assembling and installing the system and the associated price markups. Assembly and installation were handled in the same manner as the balance of system costs. The expected markup or profit margin was a percentage addition to the total of the three major cost categories. The sum of cost plus profit is an estimate of the total price to the customer.

Summary

No one will deny that cost estimation is one of the crucial steps of new venture analysis. The problem with cost estimation is that most managers and analysts understand it. That understanding usually leads to excessive analysis. Most of the new venture analyses in which we have been involved spend a disproportionate percentage of their time and resources on cost estimation. For example, the senior management involved in one new venture spent approximately $50,000 on preliminary market research (conducted by consultants to the company), no money on a competitor assessment (even though the industry was different from those traditionally served by the company), and $3.5 million on generating the cost estimate. The preparation of the cost estimate did entail preliminary engineering of the entire production process. In another example, approximately 80 percent of the total funds available for analysis were spent in support of the cost analysis, while the remaining 20 percent addressed markets, competitors, uncertainty, and finance.

In both examples, the new venture's primary strategy was not cost leadership. Rather, early market acceptance of the product was the crucial factor and consumers were not particularly price sensitive. What explains such apparently obvious misallocation of new venture resources? We believe the answer lies in the cultures of the firms. In both cases, the parent organizations were engineering firms with extensive cost estimation departments. They typically compete for large government contracts that are based on engineering quality and cost. Traditional markets are defined by a small number of customers who issue extremely detailed requests for proposals prior to purchase. Competitors in these traditional markets are limited and well known. Often, the competition has been reduced to two, three, or four firms before a major government purchase is made. All competitors have relatively equal quality engineering staffs (movement of talented engineers from one competitor to another is extensive). Cost is often the key discriminator among such firms. Unfortunately, the new ventures these firms were entering did not share the characteristics of their traditional markets. The natural tendency within the organizations was to analyze what they knew how to analyze. The result was insufficient preparation of their new ventures for the market.

The guiding principle in new venture cost estimation is to examine in detail only the key determinants of cost. If the competitive and market analyses indicate that small cost differences will significantly influence sales, costs should be modeled in detail. If the venture's strategy relies on technical or service-related uniqueness, cost estimation can be deemphasized. Remember that the objective of cost estimation is never to design a cost accounting system.

Learning and experience curves are often the central analytical tools used in new venture cost estimation. Learning and experience curves have been observed in many industrial production situations, for entire industries, and over long periods of time. Disaggregated learning curves exist at the levels of individual inputs, processing steps, and production facilities. Numerous factors have been cited as the specific causes for the observed reductions:

1. Technological advances in product design and production processes.
2. Advances in the organization of production or management activities.
3. Economies of scale in production.
4. Increased efficiencies of labor and machines.
5. Reduced prices for inputs (which may be due to any of the above sources operating in the industries supplying those inputs).

The new venture analyst should clearly identify which factor (or factors) is believed to cause the predicted cost reductions.

Observed learning effects vary widely among industries and processes. The learning curves reported in the literature most often show reduction in unit costs of 10 to 30 percent for each doubling of cumulative production. However, costs will sometimes show no change with a doubling in production volume, or may even rise in noninflated dollars. Also, the relationships between output and price are much weaker than those between output and unit cost because the former depends on demand as well as on considerations inside the production facility.

The limitations of learning curves should be kept in mind as they are applied to new venture cost estimation. If the concepts are used within the limitations under which they were developed, they can be very helpful. Their use does introduce additional uncertainties to the venture analysis. Those and other uncertainties will be addressed in the next chapter.

8

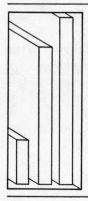

New Venture Analysis: Uncertainty

Introduction

Uncertainty is the essence of new ventures. It surrounds every aspect of the process. It keeps managers up at night. It is the spice that adds to the excitement of trying something new and different within the confines of an established firm. How do the analyst and manager capture the uncertainty of the new venture and define it well enough to manage it? We will address that crucial question in this chapter.

Uncertainty is discussed most often during key investment decision meetings with senior management. Day-to-day development and analysis of the new venture tends not to address the extent of the uncertainty; rather, the implicit objective most of the time is to reduce uncertainty. The management and staff who are committed to the venture's success find little pleasure in exploring the extent of their idea's risk.

We have observed that during new venture decision meetings, it is not uncommon for a confusion to arise between uncertainty and risk. I recall presenting an analysis of uncertainty for a new venture when a member of the executive management said, "I do not care about uncertainty, only risk." My first reaction was to question my own use of the terms. Is there some established convention within the company that I have missed? Is my perspective on the new venture lacking in some fundamental way? After brief verbal jousting, I found that the answer was negative to both questions. Some people distinguish risk from uncertainty by defining risk as only the negative aspects of uncertainty. According to their definition, risk includes only those aspects of the venture that can go wrong and lessen the economic value of the venture. Others call this "down-side risk." Uncertainty is then defined to include both risk and the likelihood that the venture will do better than predicted.

An alternative way to distinguish risk from uncertainty is by the amount of information available. An event or outcome is uncertain if you have no information on how it might turn out. In other words, you have no knowledge of the probability distribution of the outcome before it occurs. If you know something about the probabilities of various outcomes, then you are at risk rather than just uncertain. If you have gained information about the range and probability distribution of the new venture's economic outcome, you have eliminated uncertainty but not risk.

If we use the latter distinction between risk and uncertainty, new ventures must be subject to risk rather than uncertainty. It is inconceivable that the new venture's management team will have no information on the venture's outcome. Even if that condition is close to the truth, no one connected with the venture would admit it. Furthermore, the analyst could not begin his or her work without ideas about economic outcomes. When the analysis begins, it is not necessary to have any information about the ultimate economic value of the venture. It is necessary to have some ideas about factors such as the cost of product development, material and labor costs, marketing and other expenses, market size, and the final product prices that are acceptable to the market. For these reasons, we see no advantage in differentiating between the terms *risk* and *uncertainty*. We use the two terms synonymously throughout the chapter. If your corporation uses the term *risk analysis* more often than *uncertainty analysis*, use that convention.

Not all areas of uncertainty should concern the new venture. Most uncertainties or risks covered by insurance are of little consequence to the economic value of the venture. Losses of real property due to fire, theft, weather, other "acts of God," and some product liabilities are usually insurable. The key uncertainties are those that are not insurable or those factors that will damage the venture beyond what is recoverable through insurance. We have encountered many situations where losses ordinarily covered by insurance have to be borne by the new ventures. For example, the risk of death or disability of key new venture personnel can be covered by key-man insurance. However, no coverage is available if the key men quit and start a competing company. Business interruption is another risk to which the venture is sometimes exposed. Business interruption insurance can be purchased. However, there are situations that interrupt a business which this insurance does not cover. For example, we investigated a new venture dealing with a very large energy production facility. The revenue stream of the venture, which was key to its economic value, would stop if the energy produced by the facility was curtailed or reduced. One of the key uncertainties of the venture was the performance of the largely unproven technology. The venture's technical risk was not insurable. Thus, if the business was interrupted because of technical problems, claims could not be made on the business interruption insurance policy.

Most major new venture risks are not insurable, and there can be significant limitations to the insurance coverage the venture does obtain. It is always useful to determine who pays for the consequential damages to the venture if one of the insured events actually occurs: it is usually not third party insurers. Management must be careful not to depend on insurance to cover the crucial risks of a new venture without investigating the issue with insurance brokers. If the risk and its consequences are insurable, the analyst should add the cost of premiums to the recurring cost estimate and ignore it in the uncertainty analysis.

The objective of uncertainty assessment is not to find the lowest risk new ventures. Minimizing risk is inconsistent with the concept of new ventures. Abernathy and Kline (1980) discuss U.S. corporate risk taking at some length. Their major hypothesis is that modern management techniques (they would probably include venture analysis as one of those techniques) are helping managers to minimize risk but preventing them from supporting innovative ideas that lead to the creation of substantial economic value. They argue that, in the aggregate, the spread of these techniques and the practice of minimizing risk is contributing to the decline of American industry. In the new venture arena, they contend that managers have to be willing to take more risks and to try to create unique economic value in order to turn U.S. industry around. This requires longer range perspectives on profits and the ability to make decisions in high-risk settings.

The techniques we will outline below should not be construed as mechanisms that force managers away from high-risk ventures. The value of our approach is in exposing the risks to the manager. It is always useful for new venture analysts to stress the importance of risk taking when presenting risk assessments to decision makers. The analyst's job is to assure that the risks are not hidden or ignored by the manager rather than emphasizing the risks to such a degree that the manager accepts only low-return ventures to avoid them.

The decision maker's concern about uncertainty can be divided into three categories. First, s/he is concerned about the uncertainty of the results of the new venture analysis. S/he needs to know how much confidence to place in the analyst's results. Second, s/he is interested in the uncertainty of the new venture relative to competing ventures seeking the same, limited funds. Third, s/he is concerned about how the new venture relates to the broader portfolio of ventures and businesses that comprise the firm. (We will take a separate look at this third category of risk in Chapter 10.) It is appropriate to examine new venture portfolio issues only after the analysis of a single venture is complete. Thus, the first two concerns of the decision maker are treated in this chapter.

The uncertainty assessment is usually done after a baseline analysis of the entire venture is completed. An integrating framework must be put in place to combine the results of the separate market, costs, and competitive assessments described in earlier chapters. The integrating framework is the subject of Chapter 9. Why do we discuss uncertainty analysis before the integrating framework is presented? The reason is that it is important to understand how uncertainty will be treated before building the integrating framework. The integrating framework is used the most to investigate uncertainty. If that framework is not designed to address key uncertainties, it will have to be redone.

This chapter will review alternative ways of estimating the uncertainty of a single venture, primarily the use of sensitivity analysis, scenario analysis, decision trees, and Monte Carlo simulations.

Common Approaches to the Assessment of Uncertainty

All approaches to uncertainty assessment have their roots in probability theory. Any measurable element of a new venture, whether an assumption or a result of the analysis, can be displayed as a range of possible values, a range bounded by a minimum and a maximum value that the factor can attain. The range limits are sometimes established by physical constraints, but often solely by the analyst's judgment. A factor can assume any value between the minimum and maximum. However, certain values are more likely to occur (that is, they are more probable) than others. The likelihood of the factor taking on each value within the range is usually displayed by a probability curve or a frequency distribution. Figure 8-1 shows some typical frequency distributions used in new venture analysis. The simplest assumption is that any value within the range is equally probable (labeled A in Figure 8-1). Sometimes the range is divided into distinct segments (or subranges), each with a different probability. Within any subrange, the probabilities of each value are equal to all others in that subrange (labeled B in Figure 8-1). When uncertainty is handled explicitly in a

FIGURE 8-1
Simple Alternatives to the Treatment of Uncertainty in New Ventures

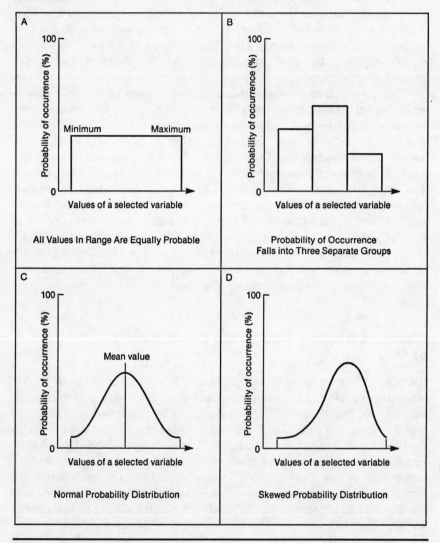

new venture analysis, the bell-shaped, normal distribution curve is usually assumed (labeled *C* in the figure). The most probable outcome is the mean or average value of the normal distribution (it is also the median and the mode). The average value should be the baseline estimate used in the venture analysis. It is then assumed that the other values are distributed normally around that average. Finally, it is possible to assume that the probability distribution of a new venture factor is skewed. The distribution can be skewed in many different ways. (An example is shown as D in the figure.)

Probability distributions are typically used to describe key assumptions of the analysis (for example, market size, recurring costs, competitor prices, competitor lead times, investment costs, required product development time, and key indicators of the economic results). The economic results of the new venture are most often measured using the internal rate of return, net present value, or return on investment. Each of these is a summary measure of economic attractiveness. That is, they reduce the total economic outcome of the new venture to a single number. We will discuss summary measures of new venture results further in Chapter 9.

Uncertainty or risk analysis is the investigation of the probability distributions that surround the summary measures of economic value. The approaches to risk analysis differ merely in how those investigations are conducted. We have identified three generic approaches to uncertainty assessment. They follow the categories identified by Carl Spetzler (1977) in his investigation of uncertainty analysis in traditional capital investment decisions.

The first category is the use of sensitivity analysis. Each selected assumption of the analysis is varied separately, and the resulting impact on the summary measure of economic value is recorded. The second category considers the probability distribution of each input variable and derives a distribution for the summary economic measure. This category usually uses Monte Carlo or some other type of simulation approach. The third category takes simulation a step further by trying to explicitly incorporate the firm's attitude toward risk into the analysis. The analyses become progressively more complicated as you move through the three categories. The first category is the simplest and most widely used. The third category presents particular difficulties in the new venture decision process which we will discuss later.

We will examine some specific analytic techniques within each of the tree categories. Sensitivity analysis and scenario analysis are examples of the first category. We will discuss decision trees and Monte Carlo simulations as examples of the second category, and we will close with a more generic discussion of the third category.

Sensitivity Analysis

Sensitivity analysis begins by making a single estimate of the new venture's economic value. The most probable value for each assumption should be used to create the estimate. As we mentioned earlier, these values should be the mean or average of each variable's probability distribution. Some summary measures are chosen to reflect the economic value of the venture (for example, internal rate of return [IRR]). The assumptions plus the method of calculation determine a single estimate of the new venture's economic value. This procedure is called deterministic because the summary measure of economic attractiveness can yield only one value for a given set of assumptions. The deterministic result is usually called the baseline or base case. Either all or a subset of the assumptions used in the baseline economic value calculation are then varied, one by one, to see their effect on the summary measure. The decision maker is given the baseline measure of economic value and the sensitivity analysis. S/he reviews the results and uses his or her judgment to assess the intangibles of the new venture decision. The combination of base-case results, sensitivity analyses, and personal judgment on the intangibles leads the decision maker to a decision. The key parameters subject to sensitivity analyses in most new ventures include: (1) market potential, (2) customer acceptance or product diffusion rates, (3) lead times (before competitors enter the market), (4) market share deterioration rates after competitors enter the market, (5) research and development costs and schedules, (6) initial capital investments for production and sales, (7) a variety of learning curve slopes, (8) relevant learning curve starting points, and (9) relevant expected (or feared) government and legal actions.

A few words of caution about the base-case assumptions need to be made before we proceed. The assumptions chosen for the base-case assumptions are often not the most probable or average values. The desires of the analyst or managers to obtain certain results can influence this choice and lead to a biased view of the new venture's attractiveness. Sensitivity analyses conducted around optimistic base-case assumptions are likely to make the venture look attractive. In practice, analysts and managers almost never consciously try to bias an entire analysis. They may notice one variable that has a devastating impact on the new venture and then choose a more optimistic base-case value for that variable. They may choose more optimistic values whenever there is a close judgment call by using the rationale that other assumptions in the base case are probably too conservative. The choice of base-case assumptions is an important set of decisions in any new venture analysis. There is a need to be as objective as possible in making those decisions and not to let subtle pressures within your company influence you.

The use of sensitivities to explore uncertainty is best seen through an example. We have briefly introduced this example before. A major U.S.-based company was considering a new venture to sell electricity to a large utility on the West Coast. The generation of electricity used a new technology with characteristics very different from those of typical electric generating facilities. The immediate issue was to assess the risk of constructing one of the new facilities in order to sell electricity. If the initial facility was successful, numerous others were planned to diversify the new venture's revenue base.

The summary measures chosen to evaluate the venture were the internal rate of return (IRR) and net present value (see Chapter 9). To calculate the summary measures, a detailed, computer-based model was built which predicted cash flows, balance sheets, and income statements for the life of the facility. Of course, the calculations were based on a myriad of explicit and implicit assumptions.

The above example illustrates the similarity between new venture analysis and the analysis of more conventional capital investments, although there are two important differences that should be noted. First, the time frame of the new venture analysis is typically longer than a capital equipment decision. Second, the uncertainty surrounding new ventures is more pervasive than in most conventional capital investments. However, there are exceptions to both of these generalizations.

The sensitivity analysis conducted in our example began with a selection of factors to be included. We made the list as complete as possible. It begins with a review of those assumptions that are explicitly entered into the computer model, but goes well beyond that starting point. The prime source of the remainder of the list was the original market, competitor and cost research that was conducted before the model was built. We also included the factors that our legal, tax, insurance, and financial advisers were discussing in venture meetings. The new venture analyst is in a position to answer most of the "what if" questions before they are asked. If perceptive about the venture, s/he can capture almost all the key factors in the sensitivity analysis. The variables selected for sensitivity analysis in our example included:

Capital cost overrun impacts.

Construction schedule delay impacts.

Other capital cost impacts.

Initial energy sales-price impacts.

Energy price-escalation rate impacts.

Capacity payment calculation (regulatory interpretations affecting part of the venture's revenue stream).

Capacity payment impacts (another revenue stream impact).

Impact of other clauses in the power purchase agreement.

Technical performance and equipment efficiency impacts.

Initial operation and maintenance cost-estimate impacts.

Escalation rate impacts (in operation and maintenance costs).

Major overhaul implications.

Changes in operational life.

Tax credit impacts.

Depreciation impacts (for tax purposes).

State and local tax impacts.

Debt leverage impacts.

Construction loan interest-rate impacts.

Permanent loan interest-rate impacts.

Loan duration impacts.

Insurance and syndication fee sensitivities.

Correlation between interest rates and inflation.

Correlation between revenue escalation and inflation.

Correlation between operating costs and inflation.

Each factor listed above was varied independently while all other factors were held at their base-case values. Each variable was altered by 10 percent, 15 percent, and 25 percent above and below its base value. It helps to carefully lay out the variations to be tested and to keep good records of the results. We typically number each sensitivity case sequentially and keep a master log of all the resulting computer outputs. We have also found it useful to obtain printed versions of the computer output, rather than just recording the end result off the computer monitor.

Before reviewing the sensitivity results, we collectively discuss the direction of each expected outcome. We intuitively determine whether the changes in the input will have a favorable or unfavorable impact on the internal rate of return. We also spend some time making a priori judgments about the relative sensitivity of the variables to be analyzed. This exercise prevents the new venture team from accepting the computer-based results too quickly; it facilitates a more critical evaluation. As you would expect, an extensive sensitivity analysis is also a comprehensive test of the validity of the integrating framework. It usually reveals programming errors and errors in logic. We believe that sensitivity analysis is valuable for this reason alone, even if the results are never shown to management.

Examples of the sensitivity results are presented as Figures 8–2 and 8–3. Figure 8–2 shows the sensitivities of the project's internal rate of return to one of the key assumptions of the model. The figure shows the relationship between the date of expiration of the federal

FIGURE 8-2
Sample of Sensitivity Analysis Results: Single Variable

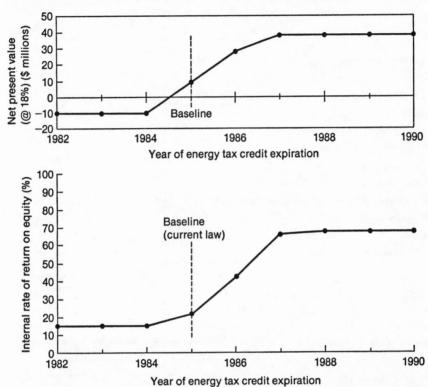

commercial energy tax credits, and the venture's net present value (top half of figure) and internal rate of return (bottom half of the same figure). At the time of the analysis, the credit was due to expire in 1985, but there was considerable discussion in Congress to have the credit extended. In this example, the venture was to be highly leveraged with nonrecourse debt. Nonrecourse debt is debt that uses some form of collateral other than the owner's credit base to secure a loan. Typical types of collateral for nonrecourse debt are the assets purchased with the loan proceeds, or the contracts between buyers and the sellers in the project. In our example, the relevant measure of economic attractiveness was the internal rate of return on the equity invested by the owners. The equity investment was the only funds at risk by the owners. By definition, the nonrecourse debt did not represent a

FIGURE 8-3
Summary of Sensitivity Analysis

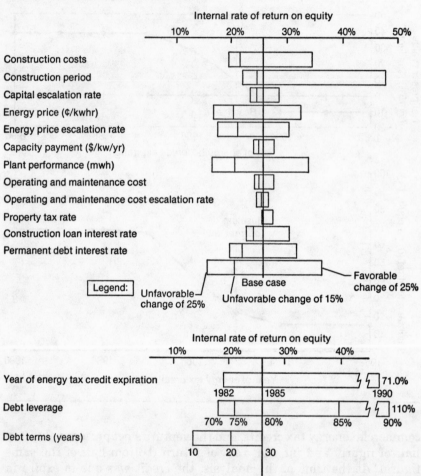

financial obligation for the owners. In most cases, internal rate of return on the entire investment should be used. (We will revisit this issue in Chapter 9.)

Figure 8-2 shows that the IRR is fairly insensitive to the tax credit if it expires on or before 1985. However, if the credit was extended to 1986 or 1987, the IRR would be dramatically increased. After 1987, the expiration date becomes irrelevant because construction of the facility would be complete. Each IRR calculated in the figure has a corresponding net present value (NPV). We assumed a discount rate of 18 percent for the NPV calculations in the figure.

Figure 8-3 shows how the entire analysis was summarized in a single chart. All the variables investigated are shown in the left column. The impact on the internal rate of return is displayed by the length of the bar on the chart. The center line represents the base-case assumption. Movements to the left of center indicate the negative impacts on IRR, and movements to the right indicate positive impacts. Only the same percentage changes to each input are displayed, so the relative impact on IRR is highlighted. As the legend indicates, a 25 percent favorable and a 25 percent unfavorable movement in each input assumption determined the end points of each bar. A 15 percent negative change was also included on each bar.

The length of each bar illustrates the importance of the variable to the new venture's economic attractiveness. A brief glance at the figure shows that factors such as operation and maintenance costs, property taxes, and capacity payments are not crucial to the new venture. The new venture's economic value could be greatly enhanced if the construction period could be shortened. However, delays in construction (from the base-case assumption) will not have as large an impact. The new venture also has a very large up-side potential return if the energy tax credit could be extended or the amount of nonrecourse debt can be increased relative to the equity injections.

In our example, the sensitivity analysis results were well received by senior management. However, sensitivity analysis suffers from some basic limitations. First, variables are changed only one at a time, and the full extent of the risk of the venture cannot be captured by looking at only one variable at a time. Second, the entire range over which a factor can vary is considered by sensitivity analysis but the probability distribution over that range is ignored. Some values within the factor's range are very unlikely, while others are quite probable. Sensitivity analysis treats all values equally. Third, the relationships among variables cannot be examined. Many variables will move in opposite directions under certain conditions. If these changes compensate for each other, the overall risk of the new venture could be less than the sensitivity results would indicate. It is also possible that one negative event could cause numerous factors to simultaneously deteriorate. The resulting decline in the IRR could be well beyond that indicated by the sensitivity results.

Scenario Analysis

Some of the limitations of sensitivity analysis can be overcome using scenario analysis. A scenario in this context is simply a group of factors or assumptions that are changed at the same time. The impact of the entire scenario is then examined in the same way that the single sensitivities were analyzed earlier. The most common scenario includes a set of variables that are affected by general economic conditions.

Two of the more common scenarios examined in new venture analyses are high inflation and low inflation. The base-case assumptions typically include moderate assumptions concerning interest rates, cost escalations, and price escalations. Different escalation rates are often used for labor and materials. Each inflation scenario contains a different but consistent set of assumptions for all these escalation rates. Similar scenarios can be developed to reflect severe or long-lasting business recessions. Scenarios of alternative market and competitor strategies within the venture's target markets also can be developed.

In the example introduced earlier, we used scenario analysis. The scenarios addressed alternative, general economic conditions. They were particularly important in the example because utility rate regulations could have delayed escalation of the new venture's revenue stream. Costs of production could rise quickly, with adjustments in revenue occurring between one quarter and one year later. This issue was not unique to our new venture. Regulatory delays have been common in the utility industry for decades. Electricity generating costs declined in the 1950s and 1960s because utilities built larger, more efficient generating facilities. Delays in rate reduction due to the regulatory process added to the profits of the utility industry. In the 1970s and 1980s, generating costs increased rapidly and the same regulatory delays added to the financial difficulties of utilities.

An example of our inflationary scenarios and their results are presented as Figure 8-4. Three inflation-driven factors are considered in the scenarios displayed in the figure. They include interest rates, revenue escalators, and operating costs. The scenarios were developed around the three factors, so that the spreads between the general inflation rate and each escalation rate remained constant. The real or noninflated rates of escalation of the three factors were not varied. Each scenario represents an internally consistent set of assumptions about inflation. The figure shows that for our sample new venture lower rates of general inflation enhance the returns to the venture's owners. Other scenarios developed in the sample new venture analysis varied the spreads between the same three factors.

Scenario analysis has its own set of limitations. First, the analyst or decision maker cannot determine which changes in factors are causing the changes in results. To sort out the causes, we must return

FIGURE 8-4
Sample of Inflation Scenario Analysis

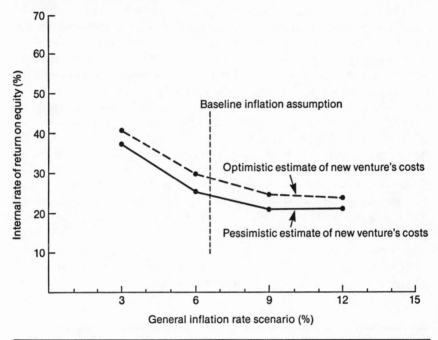

to the simpler sensitivity analysis. The impact of interactions between the input factors can be estimated only by implication—even after reviewing the sensitivity results. The second drawback is that the likelihood of a particular scenario actually occurring is still not captured in the analysis. The major advantage of scenario analysis is that the interrelationship among variables can be addressed to give a better indication of the venture's risk than a simple sensitivity assessment.

Decision Trees

Decision trees are one means of incorporating probabilities into uncertainty analysis. The decision tree concept is taken from a wider body of literature called decision analysis. A good introduction to this concept is *Decision Analysis: An Overview,* by Rex Brown, Andrew Kahr, and Cameron Peterson (1974). We use decision trees as a way of combining the probabilities of numerous probabilistic events and only one decision (that is, to invest in the new venture or not). Decision trees in our new venture analysis are a natural extension of scenario analysis. We will address decision trees again in Chapter 10 when we discuss effective communications.

The decision tree procedure, as applied to new ventures, begins by specifying probabilities for each major risk factor included in the sensitivity analysis. After the sensitivity analysis is completed, it is easy to determine the major risk factors. They are the most sensitive variables in the analysis. It is not necessary to specify a probability for each value that the factor may take over its entire range. We normally divide the range into approximately two to four subranges. We assume the probability of each value within a given subrange is equal to all other values in that subrange. The subranges divide the probability curve into large blocks or chunks. The result is a probability distribution that looks like section B of Figure 8–1 rather than section C of that figure. Next, the median or middle value of the subrange is chosen as its representative value. Figure 8–5 presents an example using three subranges. The figure shows that each subrange has its own distinct median value that is used to represent the subrange. The representative values chosen in this exercise probably will not be the 10 percent, 15 percent, and 25 percent variations used in the earlier sensitivity analysis. The new ventures analyst has to use much more

FIGURE 8-5
Chunky Probability Curve Used for Decision Tree Analysis

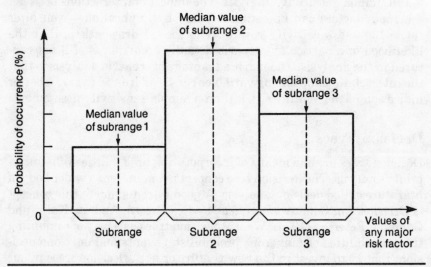

judgment to construct a decision tree. It is best if upper and lower limits of each subrange are chosen based on known facts about the market, costs, and competitors. However, many times there is not sufficient information to help subdivide the range. The analyst must then depend on his or her judgment to choose appropriate subranges.

After the chunky probability distribution is completed, the decision tree can be constructed. A sample of a decision tree is shown as Figure 8-6. The tree is read from left to right. The first stem or node is the decision to invest or not invest in the new venture. It is indicated as a small square on the tree. A positive investment decision branch is followed by all the key risk factors that have been identified. There may be other decision points in the analysis but we do not typically include them. Keep in mind that we are constructing the decision tree as an aid in the uncertainty analysis, not as a means of making the entire new venture decision.

If possible, we usually organize the key uncertain factors in chronological order. Each branching of the tree represents one of the subrange values chosen earlier. Figure 8-6 shows that the first risk factor selected in our example was the new venture's cost. We decided that cost should be divided into only two subranges. The representative values were the base-case value (originally estimated to be the most probable), and a lower cost alternative (approximately 15 percent lower than the base case).

We define a branch of the decision tree as one complete path from the left to the right side of the tree. Each branch is a combination of key risk factors much like the scenarios we discussed earlier. The decision tree in our sample contains 32 branches. The next step in constructing the decision tree is to calculate the internal rate of return (or other summary measure of economic attractiveness) for each complete branch of the tree. We assign a probability to each outcome or branch of the decision tree by multiplying the probabilities of each node or branching point along the branch. These probabilities can only be multiplied if each of the risk factors captured in the tree are statistically independent. The outcome of one factor on the tree should not influence the stated probabilities of the other events. If this is not the case, your decision tree should be revised, so the factors are totally or at least nearly independent.

When all these calculations are done, the analyst is left with a rather large array of possible outcomes for the new venture and a probability associated with each possible outcome. The only task left is to display those results graphically. Figure 8-7 presents an example of an approach we have found to be successful. To construct the figure, we organized the outcomes from least favorable to most favorable. Then,

FIGURE 8-6
Sample Decision Tree Used in New Venture Uncertainty Analysis

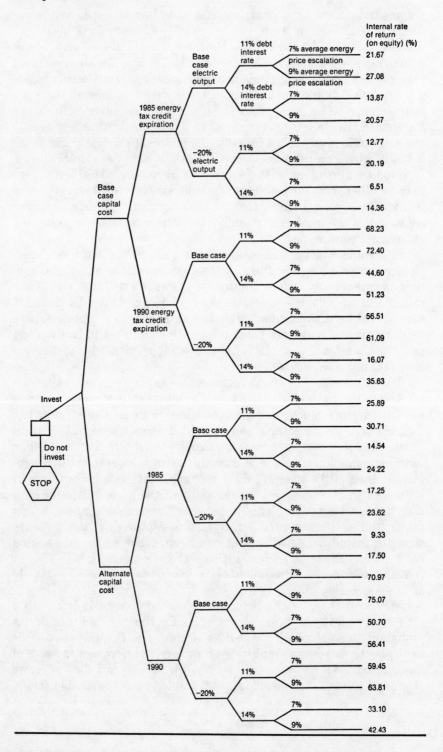

FIGURE 8-7
Sample Cumulative Probability Curve Constructed for Decision Tree Analysis

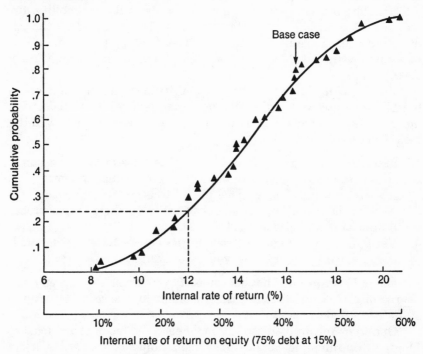

the probabilities were cumulated and graphed. The figure shows the cumulative probability of the venture's return being at or below any value read down the left side of the graph. For example, the dashed line on the figure should be read as: It is approximately 23 percent probable that the venture will achieve a 12 percent IRR or less. Conversely, there is a 77 percent (100 percent − 23 percent) likelihood that the new ventures will have an IRR above 12 percent.

Simulations

Simulations are a means of refining the chunky probability curves used in the decision tree analysis into continuous functions or functions with many small chunks rather than a few large chunks. The types of simulations we use are Monte Carlo simulations. Monte Carlo simulations involve undertaking many trials of an event (or series of events) that has an uncertain outcome. The frequency of occurrence of each outcome is recorded to estimate the probability curve of the event. In other words, Monte Carlo is a way of sampling the probability curve to understand its shape.

Simulation requires more information about the probability distribution of each key risk factor. Forecasts are gathered on the expected or average value of each major risk factors, its minimum and maximum possible values, and the shape of its cumulative probability distribution.

The difficulty in estimating probabilities for these parameters is hard to overstate. Moscato (1980), in a recent text on financial decision modeling, has provided four steps that can be adapted to assist in the task. They are:

1. Estimate the range of values that each key risk factor can assume.
2. Divide the range into a limited number of equal intervals (but more than two to four as done in the decision tree analysis).
3. Ask the new venture managers to estimate the relative probabilities of occurrence for each interval.
4. Verify that the sum of the probabilities equals 1.0 and check with the managers for consistency of their estimates.

Although Moscato does not mention it, you must also specify the degree of correlation between the variables to assure that they are statistically independent.

Once the probability distribution for each key factor is defined, the Monte Carlo sampling can begin. Random numbers are used to select which value of each key variable to use in a trial. Typically, two- or three-digit random numbers are used.

Most Monte Carlo simulations are done with computers. The random numbers are usually generated by the computer using programs that are commercially available. However, we will illustrate the process using a manual calculation. To keep the illustration simple, we will assume that only three key risk factors have been identified. We would begin each Monte Carlo trial by choosing three random numbers. The first random number would be used to select the value for the first key risk factor, the second would be used for the second key factor, and so on.

But how are the random numbers used to select those values? That is accomplished by first constructing a map or table that translates the random number into an appropriate input value. Let us assume that three-digit random numbers are being used and the first key risk factor was divided into five intervals or subranges. The random number map would look like the following:

Random numbers	Key factor's value	Probability	Cumulative probability
000–049	10	5%	5%
050–199	20	15	20
200–699	30	50	70
700–979	40	28	98
980–999	50	2	100

The number of random numbers assigned to each value of the key factor is dictated by the probability of that value occurring. When a random number is selected, the map is used to determine which of the five values of the first key factor will be used in that IRR calculation. This experiment is repeated many times. The result is a probability distribution of IRR (or any other selected measure of economic attractiveness). Confidence levels and summary statistics such as the means and variance can then be calculated if desired. The confidence levels, summary statistics, and cumulative probability distribution of the IRR are presented to decision makers to summarize uncertainty. Again, managers would use their judgment to incorporate the intangible effects and reach a decision. The mean and variance of the expected new venture results are particularly useful in comparisons across ventures. As we will discuss in Chapter 10, the variance is often used as a summary measure of risk when reviewing portfolios of ventures held by a single parent company.

A large commitment of time and resources is obviously needed to conduct a simulation on your new venture. The advantage of the simulation approach is that it allows more detailed information on the probability curves of the input variables to be reflected in the uncertainty analysis. The statistical analyses done on the Monte Carlo results provides quantitative measures of uncertainty (in the form of the variance and standard deviation of the expected economic value distribution). The disadvantage of simulations (in addition to the cost) is that your knowledge of the distributions of the input variables may not warrant the sophistication of the technique. If the input variable probability distributions are only guesses, the Monte Carlo results will be merely a combination of guesses. It may be more honest to the new venture to use an analytical tool better suited to the quality of your data. Monte Carlo simulation results may sound more impressive than simple sensitivity analysis results, but you may be doing your management a disservice by using the simulation tool.

Incorporation of Risk Attitudes

The most sophisticated or, at least, most complicated way of estimating uncertainty tries to model the firm's attitude toward risk in an abstract way prior to the evaluation of the new venture. Risk attitudes are then explicitly incorporated into a decision tree or Monte Carlo simulation. The analysis typically begins like the Monte Carlo simulation. Probability distributions of each key risk factor are estimated. Monte Carlo simulation is then used to derive a probability distribution of the IRR. The next step is to gather the risk attitudes of key corporate managers who have authority over the new venture. This is usually accomplished by asking these executives to estimate what they would pay to participate in a simple chance event with two possible outcomes. The manager or managers would be asked what dollar amount would leave them indifferent to a choice between playing the game and receiving the cash. This amount is the certainty equivalent of the game (that is, the amount they would take for certain rather than play an uncertain game). This line of questioning is continued for a wide variety of chance games whose payoffs cover the possible IRR outcomes of the new venture. The results are a mapping of economic consequences of the new venture onto an equivalent ranking of the decision maker's preferences. Using this map, the analyst translates the uncertain economic consequences of the venture into certainty equivalents. A comparison of these certainty equivalents then becomes straightforward. The final step is to present the results to the manager for review and decision. Intangibles other than risk attitudes should continue to play a role in his or her decision.

We have not been able to successfully incorporate risk attitudes into an uncertainty analysis because of at least two major problems. First, most managers and executives we have encountered do not have sufficient interest, stamina, and faith in the analyst to undergo the risk attitude collection process. Second, taking risk analysis to this level of complication is often viewed as usurping management judgments rather than supporting them.

Summary

Uncertainty analysis should play a central role in new venture analysis. The challenge to the analyst is to capture the extent and nature of the venture's risk without overemphasizing it. The techniques for assessing uncertainty come from the fields of statistics and decision theory. The new venture analyst should use his or her imagination when approaching the risk issue. The approaches we have outlined above—sensitivity analysis, scenario analysis, decision tree analysis, simulations, and the incorporation of risk attitudes—are only guidelines. The specific circumstances surrounding your new venture should be the determinant of what approaches will be most meaningful. The guiding principle of uncertainty assessment is to match the analytic technique with the quality of the data that you have available. It is usually more fruitful to spend any incremental resources available gathering better data about the key uncertainties rather than applying more detailed analytic techniques to the limited data you currently possess. We always conduct sensitivity analyses on new venture opportunities, and we usually include scenario analysis and a decision tree analysis. We rarely conduct simulations and have never been able to explicitly incorporate risk attitudes into our analyses.

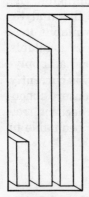

9

New Venture Analysis: Integration and Decision Making

Introduction

At this point in the venture analysis process, the analyst has gathered information on every aspect of the new venture. S/he needs a way to effectively combine that information and translate it into a few key conclusions that can be used as the basis for investment decisions. We call that process *new venture analysis integration*. In most cases, the interaction of market, cost, and competitive forces are more significant than any one factor viewed in isolation. New venture integration tries to simulate those key interactions in the process of deriving some summary conclusions.

To accomplish the new venture analysis integration, we need a conceptual framework. Such a framework serves two purposes. First, it provides a consistent way of combining all information collected in the venture analysis. Second, it provides a means of understanding how the assumptions and facts interact, and what that interaction will mean to the economic viability of the new venture.

The framework we will develop can be used to make manual calculations on the economic attractiveness of the new venture, or to develop a computer-based model for the same purpose. In our discussion, we use the term *model* in a general context to describe any explicit representation of the interactions between markets, costs, and competition. The analyst can decide whether the model should be implemented manually or with the aid of a computer. The recent improvements in software, and electronic spreadsheets in particular, make it relatively easy to develop a computer-based model. We have never developed a venture analysis integrating framework without building such a model.

We will begin our discussion with a review of the various summary measures of the economic attractiveness of the new venture that we touched on in Chapter 8. The most common of these measures include payback, return on investment, internal rate of return, and net present value. They are used with respect to the new venture in the same way that they are used to analyze more conventional capital investment decisions. Their uniqueness in a new venture setting stems from the forces that determine both costs and returns. In the next section, we will address how to integrate our completed analyses of markets, costs, and competition into the summary measure of economic attractiveness. The results of the new venture integration process are usually compiled in a business plan. Suggestions on the organization and content of the business plan are included in a later section. The chapter ends with a brief examination of the new venture decision process. The analyst's role as a communicator will be stressed in the final section.

Two aspects of the new venture integrating model are important. Obviously, the content of the model is critical. We will spend most of the chapter on that aspect. How the model is constructed is also important. We have noticed that the best integrating models are those that grow in an evolutionary way. The model begins as a very simple representation of the factors that the separate analyses in Chapters 5 through 8 have identified as important. A simple model should be completed and implemented. Sensitivity analyses should then be conducted on all factors by using the simple model. The sensitivity analysis results should be the basis for adding details and complexities to the model. Using this technique is not without its frustrations. Often, major revisions have to be made to treat key decision factors in an appropriate way. The changes can be so dramatic that it is sometimes easier to start building the entire model again rather than to revise what has already been done. During the process, it appears that an evolutionary approach is extremely inefficient, and it becomes easy to ask "Why didn't we just start with a more thorough framework in the first place and fit in the key facts as we conducted the analysis?" We have found that if this approach is used, it is likely that the new venture will be forced into an existing model rather than being the determinant of how the model will be formulated. The time, resources, and pain invested in an evolutionary model development effort are significant. But the analyst spends time only on those factors that are important to the unique new venture at hand. We believe that in the long run evolutionary model development tends to be a more effective and efficient way of integrating a new venture analysis.

Summary Measures of Economic Attractiveness

We touched on the topic of summary measures of economic attractiveness in Chapter 8. Most business analyses tend to generate a myriad of data that vary in relevance and timing. What is needed is a straightforward combination of all such data into a single summary measure that gives a clear indication of the economic value of the new venture. We have borrowed the concepts of payback, return on investment, internal rate of return, and net present value from the capital investment literature. These concepts are well known by most managers and are therefore easy to relate to other business areas of the company. They can thus be easily applied to a new venture.

The simplest summary measure of economic attractiveness is payback. Payback is defined as the number of years required to pay back the investment in the new venture with net cash generated by its operations. It is calculated by dividing the total capital investment in the venture by the average annual expected net cash flow after taxes.

Payback suffers from several serious drawbacks. First, differences in the timing of new venture investments and cash flow are ignored by the payback calculation. Second, cash generated after the payback period is achieved is totally ignored. Third, uneven annual cash flows cannot be handled except by using average annual cash flow in the calculation. Finally, payback results of new ventures are likely to be implicitly compared to payback results of conventional capital equipment investments. New venture payback periods are often substantially longer than most capital investments. Therefore, these types of comparisons should be avoided no matter which summary measure is used. The problem caused by such comparisons is most dramatic when payback calculations are made.

A slight variation to the payback measure is return on investment (ROI). We define ROI as the annual average expected after-tax cash flow of the venture divided by the venture's total investment requirements. Using this definition, the ROI is merely the mathematical inverse of the payback calculation. Others have defined ROI based on results of pro forma financial analyses. Using the latter definition, ROI is the annual net earnings after taxes divided by the total assets of the venture. A separate ROI can be calculated for each year of the venture's operation. This definition of ROI is based on accounting conventions used by the venture rather than cash flow. We have not found ROI to be a particularly useful summary measure of a new venture's attractiveness under either definition.

The best methods for summarizing the economic attractiveness of new ventures use discounted cash flows. Future cash flows are discounted to estimate their equivalent value if they were received today. The discounting of future values yields results that are commonly termed the *present value* of that cash flow. The best-known measure is the internal rate of return calculation.

The internal rate of return (IRR) of a new venture is that interest rate (or discount rate) that equates the present value of the new venture's costs with the present value of its expected after-tax cash flow. Cash flows over the entire life of the new venture are included. Differences in when cash flows occur in time are explicitly incorporated into the evaluation through discounting. Alternative trial interest rates are entered into the internal rate of return equation until the difference between the present value of costs and cash flow is zero. (See Weston & Brigham [1981] for a good reference guide to the IRR equation.)

A variation on the internal rate of return method (with some differences) is net present value (NPV). Net present value (also called the present value method) calculates a single dollar value for a new venture using the parent company's weighted cost of capital. The venture's capital requirements are subtracted from its after-tax cash flow each year. Those net cash contributions are translated to their current year equivalents using the selected discount rate and then summed. The calculation is very similar to IRR except that the interest rate or discount rate is specified in advance and the equation is solved for net present value rather than a value of zero.

Although the NPV and IRR calculations are similar, there are some important differences between them in terms of how we treat new ventures. The two measures generally move in the same direction. As the net present value (NPV) increases, the implicit internal rate of return moves above the company's cost of capital. When the internal rate of return falls, the net present value declines. The IRR approach is usually considered easier to comprehend because it gives results that are meaningful relative to those used throughout the financial world in quoting interest rates on borrowed funds, yields on bonds, and so on.

When comparing potential investments using IRR, three pitfalls have to be avoided.

1. The time horizon of the new ventures being compared must be approximately equal.
2. The relative size of the investment requirements affects the result.
3. The method implicitly assumes that distant cash flows are reinvested at the internal rate of return.

The pitfalls are most apparent when alternative new ventures are being compared. For example, a venture with an 18 percent expected IRR over a 5-year time horizon may or may not be better than one offering only 14 percent but with a 15-year time horizon. The additional 10 years of cash flow from the second venture could make the net present value of the second opportunity greater than the first, even though the IRR on the first venture is higher. It is important to use judgment, even when working with fairly standard concepts such as IRR or NPV. The Weston and Brigham text (1981) is also a good starting point for further reading in this area.

To be complete and accurate, all new venture comparisons using IRR should be based strictly on cash flows. Only cash can be reinvested or paid out as dividends. Net income on an accounting basis can be quite different from actual cash earnings for several reasons including: when revenue is recognized, depreciation and other noncash charges, capitalizing or expensing various cost items, and deferred taxes. Interest charges should not be considered a cash outflow because interest is implicitly included by the discounting procedure. Taxes are considered an outflow and should explicitly enter the venture's yearly cash outflow estimates.

An Integrating Framework

Selection of one of the commonly used measures of economic attractiveness is not the end of the new venture integration process. The challenge is to translate all the information that has been gathered into a set of meaningful assumptions for use in the IRR or NPV calculation. In other words, all the market, cost, and competitor information gathered has to be ultimately factored into the cash flow projections. After that, it is simple to translate the cash flows into NPV or IRR estimates.

We have found that the most straightforward way to accomplish new venture integration is to construct a model that estimates the behavior of the venture in its marketplace year by year for 5 to 15 years. The model must consider the dynamic interactions between buyers, competitors, and costs to be of value. The modeling begins with an initial price of the new product or service and an estimate of the quantity demanded in the first year. As time passes, the price may fall or rise due to cost trends and competitive actions. Demand will increase as prices decrease but it may also change due to prices of substitute goods, new products introduced, or changes in the preferences of buyers.

Figure 9-1 illustrates how we accomplish new venture integration. The figure shows that three primary forces enter the market place: the buyers, the venturing firm, and the competition. Legal and regulatory forces could be added to that interaction as constraints on behavior if

FIGURE 9-1
Details of Suggested Integration Model Structure

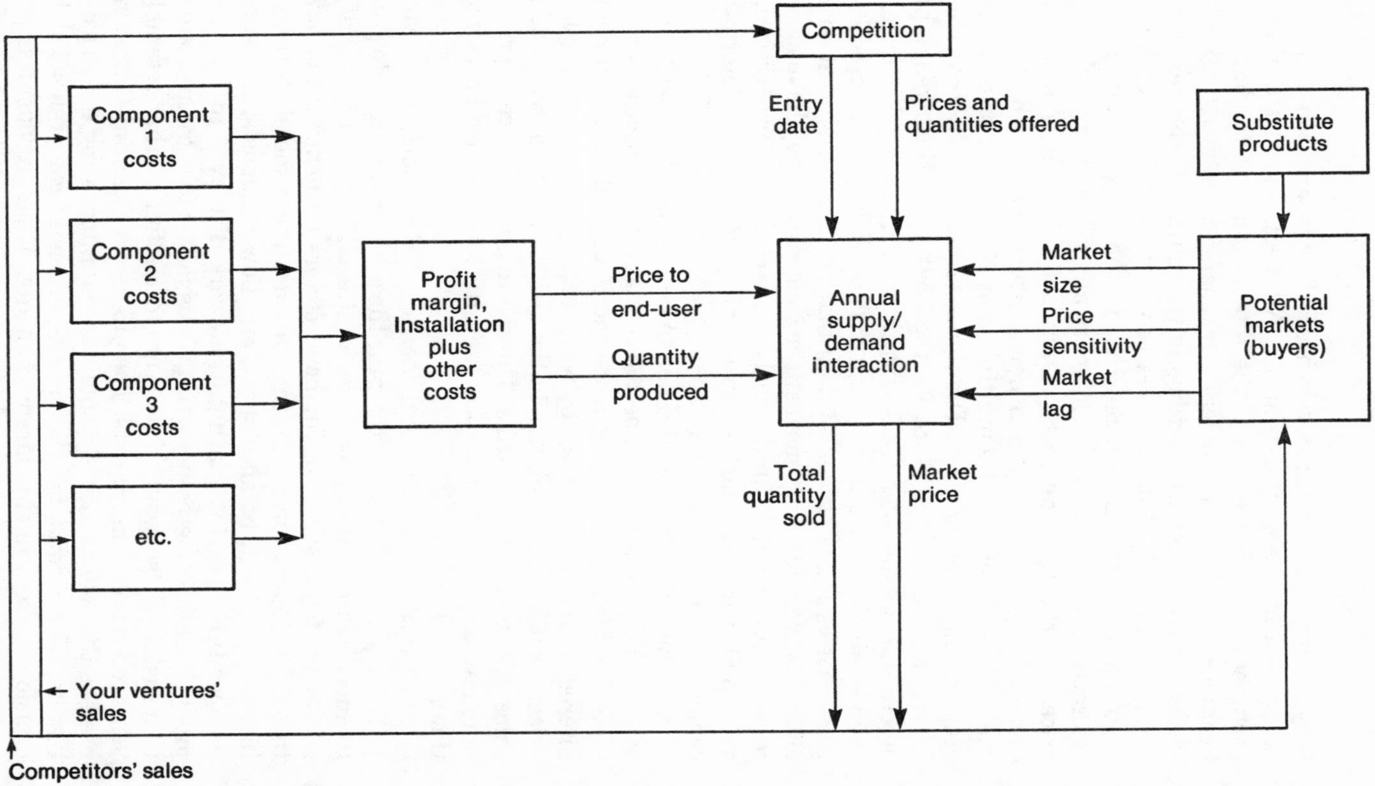

they are important to the new venture. The interaction of these forces is modeled in one-year increments. All forces interact in the market each year, and the results of the interaction lead to changes in the behavior of each of the players. The changes are made and then the model assesses their interactions in the market in the next year.

To better understand the year-to-year interactions, let us examine Figure 9-1 in more detail. Starting in the middle of the figure, the interaction of buyers and suppliers in any given year yields a market price and the total quantity of product sold. The quantity sold is divided between sales by your new venture and sales by competitors. The quantity of your sales multiplied by the market price yields your gross revenue for the year. The figure shows that the next step is to determine the offering price for the next year. Next year's price is determined by the sales of the current year, the cost of materials, and your strategic decisions on pricing. The likely price offered by competitors is estimated based on their market share, their cost structure, and probable retaliatory moves. The competition may have no product to place on the market in the early years of the venture. Current year sales and prices of your venture have to be used to determine the competitors' likely entry date.

The buyer's behavior also has to be estimated for each year (it is displayed on the figure). Expected changes in preferences, or prices of other products can be used to decide if market potential should be altered with time. The lag between economic viability (that is, the price of your product relative to the next best alternative) and actual sales can be varied with time. The relative importance of price to the purchase decision (that is, price sensitivity) can also be varied with time.

The model estimates and stores all the yearly sales volumes, prices, and cost results. We combine these yearly results into pro forma financial statements for the new venture. Pro forma financial statements are forecasts of all financial factors influencing the new venture. The factors commonly included are those found in the annual income statement, balance sheet, and flow of funds statement of the new venture. The integrating framework displayed in Figure 9-1 is producing all the necessary data. We usually add a group of submodels to translate those results into a pro forma format that resembles the venture's accounting reports. The pro forma financial statements are used as the sole means of displaying the integrating model's detailed results. The format for the results is easily comprehended by the decision makers in the parent company. Standard business analysis techniques such as ratio analyses can be conducted and specific cash flows of the new venture can be extracted from the statements. The cash flows are used to calculate the venture's IRR and NPV. The uncertainty analysis techniques described in Chapter 8 begin after the IRR and NPV calculations are derived from the pro forma results.

Numerous variations can be added to the basic integrating structure. One possible variation is the addition of a submodel to handle constraints on capacity expansion. A new venture may be faced with a situation of sales growth that exceeds planned additions to production capacity. A bottleneck may arise in the basic production capacity or the distribution channels and retail network. If such a situation is possible, it may be useful to add it to the model's capacity. We have addressed the problem by adding a supply disruption factor to some of our models. The disruption factor can be triggered by some indicator of annual sales growth. For example, total production in the previous year compared to total production in the current year is a convenient measure of sales expansion. The ratio between the two is then related to an index of cost reductions expected in the current year. The relationship can be shown by a table or a simple graph. Figure 9–2 is an example of such a graph. It relates the ratio of sales expansion (horizontal scale) to the disruption in expected cost reductions (vertical scale). The disruption in expected cost reduction is handled by estimating the proportion of units on which learning occurs in the year. The

FIGURE 9-2
Example Variation of Integrating Model—Cost Reduction Disruptions

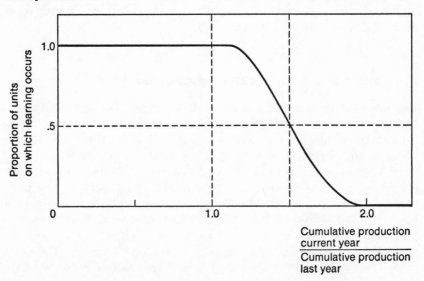

Cumulative production current year

Cumulative production last year

example in the figure shows that only half of the production expansion would be subject to learning curve effects if annual sales increased 50 percent over the previous year. If sales doubled in a single year, no learning effects would impact costs.

The figure does not illustrate that the integrating model we developed for this example allowed the cumulative learning effects to be stored or saved for future use. Our rationale was that the cost reduction normally associated with an increased production level could be realized further in the future when sales expansion slowed to a more manageable level. Learning curve effects were not lost by the disruption factor, only postponed. It would be just as appropriate to relate sales expansion to the percentage of annual production that reaches customers, especially if the bottleneck is expected to be in distribution channels rather than in production capacity.

Another variation is to explicitly incorporate the effect of R&D advances into the model. R&D usually continues after the venture is launched. R&D advances can lower the product's costs, increase product features, or both. It may be useful to model such dynamic possibilities. If R&D successes fundamentally change the product and are expected to occur in the near future, major capital investments may yield better returns if they are postponed. On the other hand, time may be valuable to staying ahead of competitors and creating customer loyalty.

Government incentives or regulations are another type of variation that can be added to the integrating model. These actions can take all sorts of forms. It is up to the analyst to determine the real economic impact of possible government actions and to represent the impact in an appropriate way within the model.

Preparing the New Venture Business Plan

The business plan is the summary document of the new venture. It contains the results of the integrating model displayed as pro forma financial statements. The plan summarizes the markets, costs, competitors, and uncertainty of the new venture. The business plan is far more than a final report of the new venture analysis. It is a concise statement of the venture's market strategy and includes the more subtle tactics that are often missed in quantitative analyses. The business plan should be the blueprint for implementing the new venture. To be most useful, it cannot be too long. Thirty to 50 pages is a good target length. The new venture team should refer to the document frequently to keep their day-to-day actions consistent with the overriding business strategy. The plan should be updated and revised as new information is uncovered and as market conditions change.

We suggest the following outline for the contents of the business plan:

1. Summary of the New Venture Strategy. One to three pages.

2. Product or Service Description and Status. Technical descriptions of the product or service(s) to be offered and a discussion of its position relative to similar products in the market. Also include an overview of the status of product development and future R&D plans.

3. Market Definition and Focus. Summary of the markets for the new venture and the rationale for the segments targeted for initial product offering. Quantitative estimates of market potential to be included and a review of the characteristics of buyers. The characteristics of buyers should include the importance of price, features, and willingness of buyers to innovate. The section should end with an overview of the marketing strategy to be pursued in each market segment.

4. Current and Potential Competitors. Begin this section with a review of the competitive environment in the targeted market segments (that is, industry structure). Discuss specific or likely competitors, including their financial strength and the products they offer. Discuss lead time, expected deterioration of market share, and likely retaliatory actions of competitors.

5. Organization and Management. The planned organization and management style of the new venture during its early stages should be explained. Some indication of how the organization will mature as production expands should be included.

6. Costs and Cost Trends. Summarize both the nonrecurring costs of starting up the new venture (capital equipment, facilities, and development costs) and the recurring costs of production. Explain expected cost declines over time and the underlying rationale. Assumptions for all cost estimates should be stated. This section should be kept fairly short.

7. Pro Forma Financial Statements. Income statements, balance sheets, and flow of funds statements for 5 to 15 years must be prepared. The section must also include the IRR and NPV base-case results.

Assumptions must be summarized and must be consistent with all previous sections of the plan.

8. Risk Factors. A brief section should be included that explains the major risks and estimates the impact on the venture's IRR and NPV. It should summarize the results of the uncertainty assessment.

New Venture Decision Making

All the techniques discussed in this book are aimed at assisting managers in new venture decisions. The techniques will have an impact on decision making only if (1) decision makers believe that analysis can help them make better decisions, and (2) the analyst can communicate the results of the venture analysis in an understandable and useful form. There is a growing body of evidence that suggests an increasing acceptance of the use of analytical tools to support business decisions. The analyst's role as communicator, however, is often overlooked.

Some of the leading consulting firms (for example, McKinsey and Co., Inc.) place much emphasis on effective communication of their results. They attribute at least some of their success to this strength. The analyst's own skills are the best tool to assure effective communication. This skill can be augmented by effective use of visual aids. The use of decision trees as a communicator has often been mentioned in new venture analysis studies as one of the more useful communication tools. Figure 9–3 recreates a decision tree used in a recent new venture analysis. The tree summarizes most of the key conclusions resulting from a six-month new venture analysis costing $500,000. The analysis was conducted in a public policy setting. The major decision was whether to pursue the project or not (labeled the "Go or No Go" decision on the tree). Each section of the decision tree represents a different parameter that was key to the project's net present valued (labeled "net domestic benefits" in the figure). The first parameter was the size of the markets. Four sizes were chosen for ease of communication. The next key issue was the rise in the cost of conventional technologies serving those markets. Three price scenarios were defined, each with a different rate of increase (2 percent, 4 percent, and 6 percent). Finally, R&D advances that would substantially change the nature of the product were included. The success of the R&D was treated as a yes or no situation. Each segment of the tree shows its expected probability below the line. The expected net benefits of each complete branch are shown along the right side of the figure. The decision tree format gives management a brief but complete view of the important new venture issues and their impact on the summary

FIGURE 9-3
Sample of Use of Decision Trees to Communicate New Venture Analysis Results

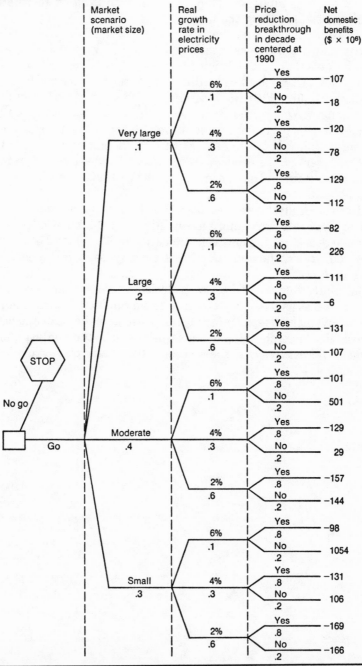

Source: D. Costello, D. Posner, D. Schiffel, J. Doane, and C. Bishop, *Photovoltaic Venture Analysis, Final Report*, 3 vols., SERI/TR-52-040, Solar Energy Research Institute (Washington, D.C.: U.S. Department of Energy, 1978).

measure of economic attractiveness. Decision trees could be developed for most venture analyses. They can easily be tailored to whatever circumstances are facing the new venture.

We are not suggesting that the analyst open his or her presentation with a decision tree as detailed as the one in Figure 9–3. The tree should be revealed in a step-by-step process. Managers must first be shown which factors are key to the new venture's success. Next, they must be presented with the alternative values that each key factor may assume. We usually show the sensitivity analysis results on each key factor in this part of the presentation and save the decision tree as a summary analysis of the new venture. If the groundwork has been properly presented, the decision tree will be regarded as an overview of the entire venture and senior management will take the time to study and understand it.

After the analyst has presented the results, the decision maker's job is to integrate this information into his own knowledge of the intangible aspects of the new venture decision. S/he should be cautious not to reintroduce factors that have already been included in the formal analysis.

The analyst must try to keep decision makers as close to the analytic process as possible while it is being conducted. Close management involvement keeps the analysis focused on the relevant issues, increases the understanding of the issues by both the analyst and the manager, and assures that the results will actually play a role in key decisions.

10

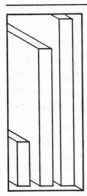

Financing the New Venture Portfolio

Introduction

The decision to pursue a new venture cannot be made without regard for the other activities of the parent company. The most relevant of those activities are the other new ventures being supported and the other capital investments under consideration. Let us turn first to the other new ventures. We believe that each new venture has to be viewed in the context of other ventures undertaken by the firm. These other ventures started at different times, developed at different rates, and are probably in different markets. The collection of all the new ventures within a firm will be termed the firm's *new venture portfolio*. A new venture portfolio has many aspects in common with a company's portfolio of current businesses. The field of strategic planning has demonstrated that attention to the interaction of a company's businesses can be key to long-term performance of the enterprise. It is logical to assume that analyzing the portfolio of new ventures can have a similar impact on their collective performance.

We have based our approach to new venture portfolios on two fields of business literature. The first is the strategic business planning literature, which examines the portfolio of businesses that comprise a corporation. The second is the finance literature, which deals with portfolios of stocks, bonds, and other financial assets. The tools and insights gained from these two fields can be adapted, in varying degrees, to the examination of new venture portfolios. The major objective of both bodies of literature is to expose the trade-offs between important but opposing factors that will influence the outcome of a business pursuit. For example, financial theory on portfolios examines the trade-off between returns and their risks. Much of the strategic business planning literature focuses on the trade-off between the growth potential of a business (or its return) and the company's ability to capture that return. Although the emphasis of the two approaches is different, the major thrust is balancing trade-offs. Trade-offs must also be considered when business managers examine the company's portfolio of new ventures. We will be presenting ways to better understand the key trade-offs within the new venture portfolio in the pages that follow.

Why should we bother with trade-offs between new ventures within the parent company? Why don't we simply pursue those with the highest economic potential? This type of thinking ignores the trade-offs that are crucial to gaining the maximum likelihood of new venture success for the parent company. A good example is again provided by the work of Wade Blackman (1973). Blackman reviews a typical situation in which a manager is faced with a limited budget to allocate to a number of competing new ventures. We can presume that the market, competitor, and uncertainty analyses have been completed and integrated to estimate the expected internal rate of return for each venture. The returns of the competing ventures are then ordered from highest to lowest. A histogram of requested funding can be developed which would probably resemble the one in Figure 10–1. Ventures are funded beginning with the highest expected IRR and proceeding sequentially toward the right side of the figure until the budget is exhausted or a corporate cutoff IRR is reached.

The above approach is used commonly in investment decisions within major companies. However, there are severe problems with this allocation procedure in the context of new ventures because it ignores key differences in risks. For example, the highest IRR ventures may be extremely risky because they are probably all in their earliest stage of product development, and most new ventures show the highest potential when they are furthest from product introduction. More information becomes available as the product becomes a reality, at which time the expected IRR usually declines. Another problem ignored by the simple ordering of returns can arise if all the ventures are in the same market or industry. One major event that significantly impacts the target market (for example, specific changes in government regulation, success of a competing technology, or changes in consumer preferences) could create losses in all the new ventures of the parent company. These are some of the reasons why venture capitalists do not choose their ventures based on a simple IRR ordering. The manager of

FIGURE 10-1
Sample Histograms of New Venture Candidates Ranked by Expected Returns

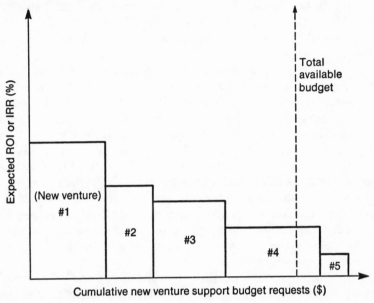

Source: Reprinted by permission of the publisher from "New Venture Planning: The Role of Technological Forecasting," by Wade Blackman, *Technological Forecasting and Social Change* 5, pp. 25–49. Copyright 1973 by Elsevier Science Publishing Co., Inc.

an internal new ventures portfolio is very similar to a venture capitalist. S/he must consider the same trade-offs that the independent venture capitalist considers. We will present some ideas on how to isolate and evaluate the key trade-offs of the new venture portfolio in the sections that follow.

The second relevant activity of the parent company which must be considered by the new venture manager is finance. The function of the firm's corporate treasury department is to obtain capital from external sources. The role of the new ventures manager is to obtain internal capital for his or her project. Logically, the two groups would not be involved with each other. The new venture manager presents requests to senior management (including the chief financial officer) who make a decision based on the venture's merits. The procedure assumes that the parent company has the financial ability to obtain the needed funds. The source of funds to implement the new venture should be a separate decision made by the treasurer and the chief financial officer.

The parent company should be investing in the new venture and not merely a conduit for outside investors who want to provide funds directly to the new venture. The firm should be using an optimal combination of operating earnings, debt, and equity instruments available to obtain the needed funds. The new venture should obtain its funds in the same manner as physical capital projects undertaken by the company (for example, buildings, factories, production equipment, or land).

Unfortunately, the way new ventures should be financed is not always the way they are financed. We have observed that most companies do support their favorite new ventures with internal financing sources. There is a second group of new ventures that falls between the lines of clearly economically attractive and clearly not viable. Champions of these latter ventures often become frustrated with the lukewarm support of the parent company. The natural tendency is to turn to financing options that relieve the company of fully funding the venture while ensuring that the venture still receives its needed resources. External funding sources such as R&D limited partnerships, joint ventures, and asset-based project financing then enter the discussion. The roles of the new venture manager and the corporate treasurer now become much closer.

We will discuss some possible sources of external new venture capital in a later section. We cannot overstress our belief that external sources should only be pursued if the parent company cannot or will not use internal funds for the venture. We must continue to remind you that the financing issue is a second-order decision, made only after the decision to pursue the venture is resolved. The new venture portfolio decision is made before the financing decision. New ventures are a special type of long-term investment made by the company. The procedures for evaluating and pursuing them should be similar to those for more routine capital projects.

Simple Approaches to New Venture Portfolio Analysis

Perhaps the simplest way to explicitly treat the critical risk and return trade-offs of alternative new ventures is to display both on a two-dimensional graph or matrix. Almost any definition of risk and return can be used to construct a matrix similar to the one shown in Figure 10-2. Point A on the figure represents the current combination of new ventures (or even a single ongoing new venture) that comprises the parent company's portfolio. The existing portfolio has some expected internal rate of return (labeled IRR_A on the figure) and some level of

FIGURE 10-2
Preferred and Undesirable Risk-Return Combinations of New Ventures

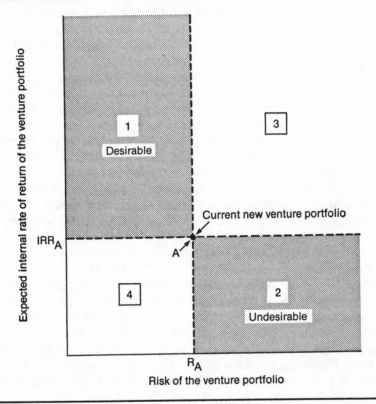

risk (designated as R_A on the figure). Any new ventures that lie in area 1 of the figure will be preferred to those in the current portfolio. Any combination in area 1 will either (*a*) yield a higher expected return than A with the same risk, (*b*) yield a lower level of risk with the same return, or (*c*) yield both a higher return and a lower risk than A. Any new venture or combination of ventures that lie in area 2 of the figure are less preferred than the current portfolio. Any ventures in area 2 will either (*a*) yield a higher degree of risk with no increase in return, (*b*) yield a lower expected return with the same amount of risk, or (*c*) result in a lower rate of return and a higher risk.

The unshaded areas of Figure 10-2 (areas 3 and 4) represent changes in the venture portfolio that depend on the attitudes of managers toward risk and return. Moving up and to the right of point A into area 3 yields higher returns and higher risks. Of course, most managers would prefer returns to increase at a much higher rate than risk. (They would prefer to be near the border of area 1.) Movements into area 3 that are close to the border of area 2 may be less desirable. Moving left and down from point A into area 4 yields portfolios with lower risks but also lower returns. Most managers would prefer being closer to the border of area 1 than area 2 if their portfolio placed them in area 4. It is not possible to determine if moves into areas 3 or 4 are desirable or not. It is crucial that management knows in which direction the overall portfolio is moving as individual new ventures are added. The matrix can serve as a good early warning system for senior management of the venturing company.

The simplicity of this approach is its strongest asset. It can be constructed using opinions about the risks and returns of individual new ventures or using some creative, quantitative measures of both factors. We have found it useful to sketch this type of matrix and experiment with alternative measures of risk and return. Informal discussions about the matrix can produce important strategic insights.

Another two-dimensional approach to examining new venture trade-offs was developed by Glen L. Urban (1968) for the examination of new product introductions. We can adapt it to the new venture portfolio issue. Urban used expected profits as a measure of return and the variation in those returns as the risk measure. Urban compares new ventures to a risk-free rate of return. The risk-free rate can be thought of as the corporation's required, minimum rate of return or the return received for risk-free investments such as the purchase of U.S. Treasury Bonds. Figure 10–3 displays Urban's matrix. The left side of the graph contains the company's risk-free rate. Higher returns from new ventures are required to compensate for added risk. There is an upward, sloping cutoff line indicating the "Go" decision and a similar downward, sloping cutoff line demarking the "No go" decision. It appears at first glance that the lower line in the figure should run straight across the graph rather than sloping downward. No one would be willing to accept greater risk and even a slightly lower return than the risk-free rate. Urban would agree with that statement. However, the line slopes down due to practical limitations on the fidelity of the expected return and risk estimates. If the return estimates of two new ventures are fairly close to the same value, it may take further investigation to determine if the original estimates were reasonable. The wedge-shaped shaded area of Urban's graph represents the uncertain region where it will pay to spend time gaining more information about a new venture before making a positive or negative decision. The key problem that must be solved is the slope of those two lines for your company and the riskless return that is applicable. Displaying all the

FIGURE 10-3
Urban's Risk-Return Matrix

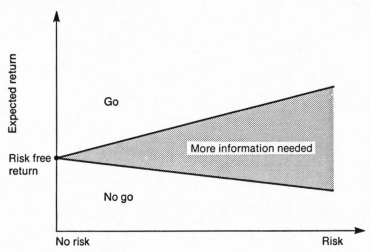

Source: Reprinted by permission of Glen L. Urban, "A New Product Analysis and Decision Model," *Management Science* 14, no. 8, April 1968. Copyright 1968, The Institute of Management Sciences.

ventures on this type of matrix again shows what type of profile the collection of new ventures is producing.

There is obviously a close relationship between Figures 10-2 and 10-3. Both figures show new venture returns and their associated risks. The major difference is whether the venturing firm considers the relevant starting point to be a risk-free investment or its current portfolio of new ventures.

Still other ways of displaying the key trade-offs of the new venture portfolio can be constructed by moving away from the direct measurement of risk and return. The strategic planning literature is full of examples of the creative use of two-dimensional matrixes. A recent book by Abell and Hammond (1979) provides a concise review of many of these approaches. Some of the classic matrixes (for example, the trade-off between market share and industry growth) are based on empirical observations of business performance over decades. Unfortunately, new ventures do not have this body of observation to draw upon. The new venture analyst and manager have to rely on their own intuition and innovativeness to plan what is useful to portray. A sample approach we have used is displayed as Figure 10-4.

Figure 10-4 shows a simple matrix of industry dispersion versus

FIGURE 10-4
Sample Matrix of New Venture Development Stage versus Type of Market Addressed

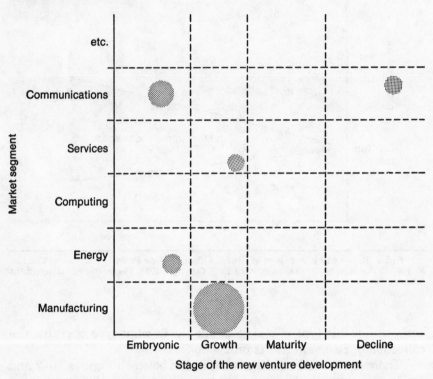

stage of the product development cycle. Each circle on the chart represents a different venture, and the size of each circle can be used to express the level of corporate resources expended or projected for each venture. Thus, a third critical dimension is brought into the matrix. The matrix display could be used to determine whether the new venture portfolio is sufficiently diversified in these two dimensions. If the portfolio is concentrated on a small number of markets, or if most ventures are in the same stage of development, the new ventures manager may want to consider steering the portfolio in a different direction.

The two indicators shown in Figure 10-4 can be replaced by any other factors that could illustrate the diversity of the portfolio. The analyst and his or her management team are often the best judges of which indicators are appropriate for their situation.

Constructing matrixes such as these may give useful insights about a parent company's new venture portfolio. These insights are limited by a lack of empirical data on how such factors influence the success of new ventures. Thus, implications drawn from this analysis have to be based on intuitive judgment. The matrixes are most useful when they are developed and revised on an experimental basis. Certain factors can be chosen and the results reviewed by a few managers. Some insights will be produced along with ideas for new matrixes. Those new matrixes can then be built and the group can reconvene for another session. The process should continue, so that better results will evolve over time. The evolutionary approach of the simple portfolio matrix analysis can be useful in properly evaluating the new venture portfolio.

Quantitative Approaches to New Venture Portfolio Analysis

The term *portfolio analysis* is most commonly used in the field of finance. Recent advances in financial theory have led to the development of various quantitative approaches for analyzing portfolios. One of the most elegant approaches, termed the Sharpe-Markowitz model (Sharpe, 1970), was designed to analyze decisions concerning the optimal mix of stocks and bonds in a portfolio. The model uses numerical estimates of each stock's expected return and risk, as well as correlations between the risks of all pairs of stocks within the portfolio. These estimates are then manipulated within the model to derive an optimal mix. The model estimates what stocks to purchase and what percentage of your portfolio should be in each one.

We have adapted theories, concepts, and techniques from many disciplines in our analyses of new ventures. It seems reasonable and even desirable to try to borrow quantitative portfolio analysis for application to the new venture process. We have spent a considerable amount of time exploring the application of stock portfolio models to new venture portfolios. Our attempts have spanned a number of years and a variety of venture portfolios. Unfortunately, we have never been able to find a situation where the quantitative tools used in stock portfolios can be applied to new ventures. The basic problem is that new ventures do not share enough features with the portfolios of stocks and bonds. We can save the new venture manager and analyst considerable effort by explaining why we believe quantitative portfolio theory is not useful.

Let us review some of the key differences between the new venture portfolio and the securities portfolio. The most obvious reason that the portfolio model cannot be applied to a collection of new ventures is that the latter are not available in continuously divisible funding increments. The new ventures manager cannot decide to put 1 percent of the capital pool in a venture that actually needs 6 percent of the pool to reach the next development milestone. Each venture in the portfolio is wholly owned by the parent company. The decision is whether to continue to support the venture or drop it. There are certainly various discrete levels of support that can be chosen. These levels are not analogous to the investment options available if conventional stocks or bonds were being considered.

The most serious problem facing the new venture portfolio is that the level of information available on the various ventures is quite different. New ventures, in their early stages of development, are subject to an enormous level of uncertainty. With time and resources, the uncertainty is reduced and the expected returns may simultaneously increase or decrease. New ventures are not static assets that are held by a firm and then traded. There is not an existing bank of historical data relating to a particular venture's returns or risks, nor is there an empirical basis for deriving the needed quantitative estimates of expected returns, risks, and risk correlations.

Finally, the conventional financial portfolio model incorporates interactions among risks but does not investigate interactions among the expected returns. Factors such as joint production facilities, shared R&D, and shared marketing and sales costs complicate the portfolio selection problem and destroy another assumption of the conventional securities portfolio model.

In summary, we have not been able to adapt the more quantitative techniques of financial portfolio theory to the unique problems facing the new venture portfolio. The essence of conventional portfolio theory is to determine how various individual investments vary with changes in macroeconomic business cycles, and then alter the mix of investments to assure the best performance of the group as a whole. The new venture's portfolio manager must be concerned with exactly the same problem. The insights gleaned from the financial portfolio theories end here. Actual use of the quantitative aspects of those theories cannot be adapted to new venture portfolios. Thus, intuition and the simpler approaches described earlier are the appropriate tools for the new venture portfolio manager.

External Financing of New Ventures

The champion of the new venture idea within an existing company is a unique person. He or she is certainly loyal to the parent company.

Otherwise, this individual would leave the company and take the idea along rather than try to persuade the existing power structure to act outside the usual dimensions of the business. The new venture champion is also too restless and perhaps too ambitious to ignore his or her own ideas and concentrate on his or her job as it is defined. Many authors are exploring the personalities and motivations of entrepreneurs and intrapreneurs. It is not our intent to repeat or even summarize their findings. However, if we briefly imagine the thoughts of the new venture champion as s/he attempts to get support for an idea, we begin to understand the role of external, new venture financing. If the new venture champion is successful, everyone is in a winning situation. If the idea is rejected early in the selection process, the champion may feel rejected but his or her position with the company is probably unharmed. The attempt, then, should be viewed as a positive reflection on the champion's career.

The trouble really arises with the marginally attractive new venture. The idea may have received initial support to prepare a business plan or even to develop the prototype product. But economic events may have turned against the venture later in its life cycle or other ventures in the company may have overtaken it. The parent company should have a mechanism for reabsorbing these talented intrapreneurs into the business mainstream and curtailing the venture. Our experience has shown an absence of both a convenient reentry mechanism and, more importantly, an unwillingness to terminate the venture after resources have been spent pursuing it. A clear-cut decision is extremely difficult in this situation. Sunk costs should be totally ignored, but we believe managers still allow those costs to influence their decision regarding continuing or terminating the venture. Market and competitor conditions are usually uncertain and could reverse themselves quickly in the venture's favor. The new venture champion has the same or an even greater level of commitment to the project.

The most probable outcome of the marginal new venture that is under management review is a tentative decision to continue to pursue it but with a reduced level of resources. The venture's manager is in a real dilemma. The reduced support is usually viewed as a guarantee of failure. Thus, financial support becomes the focus of the manager's efforts rather than the new venture's target market. The personality type of the intrapreneur is creative enough to begin to explore alternative ways of obtaining support.

The problem can be simply stated. How can the venture obtain more financial resources without costing the parent company more money? The only possible answer is to use someone else's money. The intrapreneur who reaches this conclusion will try next to externally finance his or her internal new venture.

We argued strongly in the opening pages of this chapter that the most appropriate way to finance internal new ventures is to use the firm's conventional sources of capital funds. Do not seek special outside financing sources except as a last resort. The manager of the marginally attractive new venture is usually looking for funding of last resort. In some cases, external financing is justified and can be profitable for all involved parties. In others, the pursuit of such options requires such an extraordinary amount of senior management time and attention that it would probably have been more efficient to simply terminate the venture earlier.

The pages that follow briefly review a few of the possible external financing vehicles that are available. The discussion should serve as a menu of possible sources for use by the intrapreneur seeking financing of last resort. Most of the external financing vehicles are at least partially driven by tax incentives for investors and by what is in vogue within the financial community. Thus, the options available to the intrapreneur and their costs change rapidly (and are rapidly changing).

We suggest contacting (through the treasurer's office) your company's investment banker if external financing is being considered. Bankers routinely recommend that they should be involved from the early planning stages of the financing process. That advice is worth following. However, most medium- to large-sized existing firms have the legal, tax, and financial talent available to do a great deal of the early financial engineering. Internal assistance should be used before you attempt to get approval for external advisers' fees.

There are three basic principles to keep in mind when considering the use of external capital. First and foremost, the circumstances surrounding the new venture should dictate which vehicle is appropriate. The stage of product development, the venture's sales history, the amount of capital funds needed, and the objectives of the parent company are the factors of most relevance. Do not become focused on a particular financing vehicle before you investigate all options. In many cases of successful new venture financing, numerous financial instruments are used simultaneously. For example, common stock, preferred stock, nonrecourse debt, subordinated debt, and convertible debt might all be used to finance a single new venture. Unnecessarily large amounts of ownership or control of your venture can be given away if the financing vehicle is chosen too early.

A corollary to the first financing principle is to explore in some detail the real objectives of the parent company regarding the new venture. Are they just trying to rid themselves of the capital requirements, with only a secondary interest in maintaining a large equity position in the venture? Do they just need external assistance to overcome one large development cost expenditure, but want to control the venture after that stage? Do they want to maximize the current cash proceeds from divesting the venture or are they willing to wait for longer term returns? These types of questions are fundamental. However, we have found that many senior managers have difficulty determining their objectives in this situation. The new venture management team has the responsibility to press the senior management for guidance in this area, for it is rarely offered in a distinct and consistent manner. Internal and external financial, legal, and tax advisers are expensive. A tremendous amount of time and resources can be wasted if the parent company's objectives are not well understood before these advisers are retained.

The second basic principle regarding use of external, new venture capital is to carefully assess the real costs of each financial instrument. Do not stop with an analysis of the near-term costs. Consider one or two long-term futures (one with a highly successful product and one with a market failure) and then determine the total cost of the deal. You may find that the vehicle you have chosen has given the venture's up-side potential to outside investors and left your company with only the risks. Alternatively, the venture could be left with very large debt service requirements that are fixed costs to the venture. If the venture experiences a modest economic recession without a corresponding rapid fall in interest rates, the firm can become insolvent. A final example is the situation where the venture gives away too much equity in its initial bid for external capital. When the next financing phase occurs, the firm needs more capital but has little equity left to sell. Intrapreneurs can be left with a minor equity position after the second financing phase has been completed. This small ownership position can, in turn, seriously erode their personal commitments. All these examples highlight the need to thoroughly assess the long-term costs of any external financing vehicle being considered.

The third basic principle regarding use of external capital is to do some shopping. Any financing source will be interested in your venture if you are willing to give away the majority of ownership for a nominal cost. The best deals occur when your objectives are well matched to those of the external financing source. All types of financial institutions, individuals, and nonfinancial institutions participate in new venture financing. Venture financing does not have to be restricted to national boundaries. International investors may share your attitudes about the venture, even though domestic firms are not interested. Your investment banker should be able to identify the most promising potential investors, but s/he may also have a limited perspective based on the organization's traditional client base. We have found it useful to shop for investment bankers first and then to work with the banker of your choice to shop for the appropriate external investors.

With these three principles in mind, we will examine a sample of the currently popular financing vehicles. The first is the research and development (R&D) limited partnership. We will review it in some detail to give a flavor for what factors determine the appropriate financing vehicle. We also hope to demonstrate how the structure of the vehicle is driven by current tax laws and the interpretations of those laws in tax courts. We will also review venture capitalists, joint ventures, and project financing. The chapter will end with an overview of other financing vehicles available.

At the time of this writing, the R&D limited partnership is undergoing some strong legal tests and rumors of congressional action on the subject are being heard. This situation is common in the dynamic arena of innovative, new venture finance. Our review is not intended to provide a prescription for conducting new venture finance. The combined legal, tax, and financial talents of your company, and perhaps those of outside advisers, are required to plan and implement almost any external, new venture financing.

Research and Development (R&D) Limited Partnerships

The research and development limited partnership is a financing vehicle designed to provide funds for early development requirements of a product-oriented new venture. It is a means of raising external funds for a new venture's R&D without compromising the parent company's (1) overall credit rating, (2) exposure to R&D risk, and (3) technical or managerial control of the project. The approach also accelerates the returns and tax benefits to the external R&D investors over most conventional investment vehicles, thus enabling investors to take R&D risks that would normally be unacceptable. Almost all expenditures that directly lead to the development of a new product or a significant improvement in current products can qualify for the favorable tax treatment used in the R&D partnership.

A limited R&D partnership is comprised of both general and limited partners. The parent company must form some type of separate legal entity to serve as the general partner (for example, a subsidiary). The subsidiary would contribute the development idea and actually conduct the research. The limited partners would be external investors (individuals) looking for tax benefits and attractive long-term capital gains. The limited partners contribute the required funds after signing an R&D contract. The R&D contract specifies the repayment schedule, work breakdown schedules, milestones, and other provisions typical of R&D contracting.

A sales or option agreement is signed at the same time as the R&D contract. The sales agreement states that if the R&D is successful, the new venture company has the option to buy all rights to any inventions in exchange for royalties based on gross sales of the resulting products. The limited partners bear all the R&D risk. They also bear some marketing risks because royalties are based on sales (not just meeting R&D goals). The new venture company bears some risk of cost overrun because royalties are independent of the company's profit margin or total earnings. The sales agreement is constructed in that manner to assure that both the returns to the limited partners are taxed as capital gains, and their cash flow occurs soon after the product is commercially sold. If the investors had contributed conventional equity, their cash flow would not occur until the new venture corporation had enough earnings to declare a dividend.

The sales agreement may contain two other provisions. First, the new venture company can sometimes put a ceiling on the royalties to be paid. Once the ceiling is reached, the company has no further obligation to the limited partners. The ceiling amount is quite high and is based on the risk of the R&D project relative to the returns of alternative investments. There may also be a minimum royalty payment included to give the new venture company incentive to market the product.

The R&D limited partnership currently takes advantage of two important tax benefits. First, the limited partners can immediately deduct their R&D contributions from their taxable income. R&D expenditures are appropriate tax deductions, even though the new venture has not yet offered any product for sale. Second, if the partnership is correctly structured, the royalties received by the limited partners may be taxed at the lower capital gains tax rather than as ordinary income.

The implementation of an R&D limited partnership can only be accomplished if a specific set of development activities can be identified by the new venture. New ventures in this situation should prepare a separate business plan around the R&D effort. The business plan should include (1) an assessment of technical feasibility, (2) an analysis of markets and potential sales, and (3) an analysis of financial returns and risks to the limited partners.

If the new venture business plan is already completed, the documents needed to approach an investment banker with an R&D limited partnership are much easier to assemble.

Storage Technology Corporation (STC) raised $50 million in 1981 using an R&D limited partnership. The money was to be used to develop, manufacture, and market a large-sale, high-performance computer that would compete with IBM. The general partners were two subsidiaries of Storage Technology Corporation. STC Computer

Research Corporation conducted the research and managed the project. STC Computer Finance Corporation pledged to contribute up to $10 million if the R&D limited partnership offering was undersubscribed. STC Finance also provided some working capital loans and agreed to make other project loans to assure that the project was successful. Expected after-tax annual returns to the limited partners were over 40 percent at the time. After development was completed, STC had the option to enter a joint venture with the partnership to manufacture and market the computers. The limited partners were promised a percentage of the profits on initial sales and a declining royalty percentage on sales of later units.

In 1983, STC attempted to raise additional capital for the project using the same mechanism. Soon after the second offering, the entire project was canceled. As expected, litigation ensued and the court decisions are still pending.

In general, the financing costs of an R&D limited partnership are high in terms of future profits from R&D. However, the mechanism can be useful if (1) the R&D has significant technical risk, (2) sales of the resulting product/technology are uncertain, and (3) no lower cost R&D funding sources are available. Internal sources of funds from the parent company will be much less expensive than the R&D limited partnership.

Venture Capitalists

Venture capital is currently a booming industry in the United States, although signs of slower growth are beginning to emerge. Ways to secure venture capital are written about in numerous periodicals, books, and symposiums. A brief visit to the local bookstore will uncover many of these information sources.

Venture capitalists are usually partnerships that raise a pool of funds using public or private offerings. Venture capitalists then invest these funds in a portfolio of start-up companies with the objective of earning large returns. Venture capitalists usually provide funds to start-up companies in return for a significant share of the company's ownership (stock). The percentage ownership required by the venture capitalist depends on the amount of funds required and the business outlook for the company. Percentages between 10 percent and 65 percent of the starting company are possible. Venture capitalists become actively involved in the start-up company and will redirect it or even replace senior management if they believe it will enhance the company's likelihood of success.

There are hundreds of venture capital partnerships in the United States. These partnerships often specialize in particular industries, geographic areas, or both. The objective of the venture capitalist is clear: s/he wants to gain high returns on his or her investment in a moderate period of time (three to five years), and is willing to accept a large amount of risk in the pursuit of these returns. The risk is lowered by diversifying the capital pool into a portfolio of new ventures.

Venture capitalists can be appropriate sources of external capital if the parent company does not want to maintain a controlling interest or a dominant ownership position in the new venture. We have witnessed the use of a venture capitalist in a small new venture in the Southwest United States. The new venture was nurtured within a medium-sized, highly successful electronics firm. Market conditions for the venture's products did not materialize and the parent company was no longer interested in the venture. The venture's intrapreneurs were committed to it and they convinced the parent company to allow them to obtain external capital. The employees bought some of the equity in the new venture, but the majority was sold to a venture capitalist. The parent company retained a minor equity position. The net result was that the key personnel held only minimal equity and had substituted management control by the parent company for management control by the venture capitalist. The objective of the parent company may have been well serviced by this arrangement (to painlessly divest the venture and get some cash out of it), but the goals of the key intrapreneurs were seriously compromised. It is yet to be seen whether the venture capitalist will be as patient with the new venture as the parent company.

Joint Ventures

Joint venture is a loosely defined term that applies to any business endeavor collectively undertaken by two or more firms for a specific business purpose. Joint ventures can take the form of new corporations in which equity is shared between the venturing firms, or they can be unincorporated arrangements that merely represent collectively agreed upon actions.

Alternatively, the venturing companies can form a partnership and the term joint venture still may be used. Joint ventures are not a financing vehicle in the usual sense but they can be used to help your new venture obtain needed funds, services, or expertise. If your new venture faces a financial problem, a joint venture could be arranged in which your parent company provides the technology and know-how while other venturing firms provide capital for development. It is logical to look for coventurers who can also contribute to other crucial aspects of the new venture. For example, an existing firm with a well-established sales and distribution network in your target market may be a prime candidate. A joint venture partner with superior production skills may also be a good match for a firm with good development capabilities but limited production skill.

Joint venture is an imprecise term in the sense that it can take all types of forms and involve a wide variety of companies. Look to product suppliers, distributors, and other associated businesses as initial coventurers. Your management's objectives and the requirements of the new venture should be the key determinants of how a joint venture is arranged.

Satellite Business Systems (SBS) is a good example of a new venture financed through a joint venture. SBS is a joint venture partnership among Aetna Life and Casualty, COMSAT General Corporation, and IBM. The objective of the new venture was to provide advanced, high-volume, satellite-based communication services to major corporations around the world. IBM supplies some of the equipment used in the system and was an early subscriber. COMSAT has the required satellite communications experience, and Aetna brings financial resources and knowledge of some user needs. All three partners have equal interests in SBS. Their total investment over the past 10 years is over $1 billion. Each coventurer bought equity to and held debt in SBS. In 1981, all the debt was converted to equity. SBS is now a major force in the rapidly growing communication satellite industry. However, its market segment (that is, business communications) is not developing as rapidly as expected and SBS has not yet produced much profit. Thus, SBS remains a high-risk venture with the possibility of large returns.

Project Financing

Project finance is another general term referring to any financing vehicle that is based on the assets of a project rather than the credit worthiness of a project's participants. The intent of project finance is to allow an individual project's assets to provide the collateral for debt without seriously eroding the parent company's ability to obtain future credit. (A particularly good introduction to project finance can be found in Chrystie & Fabozzi, 1983.) Project financings are usually arranged in connection with joint ventures for large construction projects (for example, pipelines, port facilities, or ships).

A new venture is not a capital asset that can be used as the basis for a project finance. However, the products built by the new venture may be used in project financing. One situation where we saw the possibility for using project financing involved a new product that had completed its development cycle but had made no sales. The product (a commercial-scale, energy production system) represented a large capital investment by the customer. The high capital cost was one barrier to early sales. Project financing was considered as a means of making the initial sales. The project was large enough so that a sale would create enough working capital and backlog to assure the financial success of the new venture. In this circumstance, project financing was indirectly used as a means of providing external funding to the new venture. Project financing can only be used in extremely special new venture circumstances.

Other Financing Vehicles

There are many more financing vehicles available to the new venture seeking external funding. In fact, the ones described above may represent some of the more unusual financing vehicles available. The more common vehicles involve the issuance of equity, debt, or both. In 1984, one of the more popular vehicles was the leveraged buy-out. Leveraged buy-outs can occur when the parent company is willing to sell an internal venture to selected employees. Many leveraged buy-outs currently being arranged address aging ventures or product lines of the parent company rather than new ventures. The same mechanism would be used whether dealing with a new venture or a parent company's repackaged old product line. The employees (usually the new venture's intrapreneurs) typically do not have the financial resources necessary to acquire the venture. In that case, they could arrange to buy the venture using a nominal amount of their personal funds, with the remainder coming from borrowings. The debt could be issued by the newly formed venture company and the proceeds then given to the parent company. The intrapreneurs end up with a majority of the new venture's stock but the company is immediately burdened with a large amount of debt. The expense of servicing the debt is a large fixed cost to the new venture company. Early fluctuations in the venture's revenue stream could produce severe, short-run cash flow problems.

Leveraged buy-outs are more commonly used to take a publicly traded company into private ownership. The management of a publicly traded company borrows (through the company) the funds needed to purchase the outstanding stock. The result is again a large debt burden for the company, but ownership control is placed in the hands of the venture's management.

Leveraged buy-outs are only one vehicle that uses traditional debt and equity vehicles in creative ways. Your financial advisers and internal finance experts can probably identify other possible vehicles to fit your new venture's needs. The new venture arena is fertile ground for creative financing. It should, however, remain the financing source of last resort to the internal new venture.

11

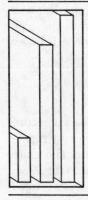

Summary and Potential Pitfalls

Introduction

The motivation to launch a new venture within an existing company comes from the realization that your firm's current product lines will not fulfill your long-term sales and profit goals. We have defined new ventures to include any segregated activity within an existing firm that is devoted to the exploitation of a novel situation. The products arising from new ventures are significantly different from the firm's current lines, serve different customers, or both.

Uncertainty is the hallmark of new ventures. There is uncertainty about the product research and development effort, the technical performance of the product in the field, its production costs, the viability of its markets, the actions and reactions of competitors, and the regulatory climate to which your venture will be exposed. Finally, there is the uncertainty of whether the parent company can maintain the organizational flexibility needed to sustain the new venture. Analytical tools developed in other disciplines can be of assistance in launching new ventures. They are aids to clear thinking in the uncertain world of new ventures.

The ultimate goal of every new venture must be the creation of economic value for the owners of the venturing firm. All aspects of a new venture analysis must try to evaluate the venture's likely contribution to the economic value of the parent company. We have organized the process of evaluating the economic value of new ventures

FIGURE 11-1
New Ventures Decision Analysis Framework

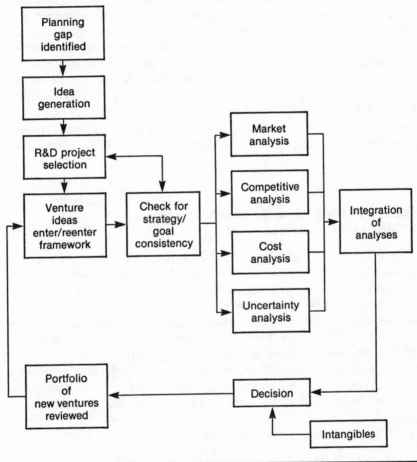

into a structured framework: Figure 11-1 presents that framework. All the market, competitor, cost, and other research conducted in pursuit of a new venture should fall within this framework. Most of the blocks contained in Figure 11-1 are the subjects of separate chapters. We will summarize the techniques that can be used to accomplish each of the blocks in the figure and provide some guidelines as to what should and should not be done in each step of the new venture analysis process. Most of the pitfalls we have encountered in conducting new venture analysis can be avoided by following the guidelines.

Strategic Plan Review
(Discussed in Chapter 1)

The need for new ventures is usually discovered when the parent company is engaged in a formal or informal strategic planning exercise. Projections of current business operations may show that growth in sales or profits is less than the firm had projected. We term the difference between desired growth and projected growth a *planning gap*. Review your strategic plans to determine if your procedures are adequate to identify a planning gap that may arise 5 to 15 years in the future. If your procedures are adequate to detect such a gap, take some time to explore the planning results to see if a gap may occur. If you do identify a planning gap, new ventures should be considered as a possible solution.

New Venture Idea Generation
(Discussed in Chapter 3)

New venture ideas are needed to begin to fill the planning gap. Idea generation requires an expansive view of the future needs of consumers and of future trends in technology. Creativity is the most important requirement for this part of the new venture analysis process. We have reviewed a number of techniques available to help stimulate and channel that creativity. These techniques include: trend extrapolation, Delphi forecasting, cross impact analysis, brainstorming, Synectics, focus groups, factor analysis, and a variety of informal approaches. None of these techniques involve a passive role for management. New venture ideas need to be actively sought out and rewarded by the parent company.

When generating new venture ideas:

DO

- Make idea generation a creative process within your company.
- Involve a wide variety of company personnel and use idea generation as a staff motivator.
- Use numerous idea generation techniques including market oriented surveys and technology oriented approaches.
- Establish an appropriate reward system for employees who generate promising new venture ideas.
- Involve departments not usually associated with research and development (such as finance, administrative groups, quality assurance, production operations, and customer service).

- Include meetings where the R&D department is exposed to the marketing group and vice versa.

DO NOT

- Rely on passive means to gather new venture ideas within the company.
- Depend solely on market or customer surveys as the source of new venture ideas.
- Allow criticisms or judgments to be made on new venture ideas until the idea generation cycle is completed.

Research and Development Project Selection (Discussed in Chapter 4)

Funding research and development (R&D) projects is often the first time that a measurable amount of the parent company's financial resources have to be committed to new ventures. R&D can be the first step to launching a new venture. Most of the analyses done before the new venture is commercially introduced should also be done before R&D projects are started. The main difference between the two analyses is the quality of information available. Although R&D project selection is shown as a separate block in Figure 11-1, each of the analyses listed on the figure is first done for R&D projects and later redone when larger capital commitments are needed.

There have been hundreds of R&D project selection models described in the business literature. We have developed a relatively simple scoring method for such project selection that works well. The procedure begins with senior management providing some strategic directions regarding the relative priorities of various business sectors. Middle management then selects surrogate measures of market potential, costs, competition, uncertainty, and scientific merit. R&D project ideas are generated by the scientific staff and then rank ordered using the above surrogates. Senior management makes the final decision on the projects that will be pursued.

When selecting research and development projects:

DO

- Establish a formal but flexible approach to R&D project selection.
- Keep the selection approach as simple as possible.
- Involve senior management in issues of overall R&D direction; middle management in selecting specific projects; and the research staff in creating research ideas and obtaining results.

- Build an R&D project selection approach that will allow more information to be added as it becomes available.

- Take the needs and motivations of your research staff into account when selecting R&D projects.

- Remember that R&D is only successful if it eventually adds economic value to the firm.

- Link the R&D selection process to the firm's larger strategic planning process.

DO NOT

- Allow R&D selection models to be a substitute for good management judgment.

- Use quantitative approaches to R&D project selection that require more or better information than can be reasonably gathered.

- Focus all R&D projects on a single market segment or technology.

- Allow all the company's R&D projects to be in the same development stage (for example, they should not be all scheduled for completion in the same year).

- Allow R&D budgets to be changed based on the near-term profit performance of the parent company.

Market Analysis (Discussed in Chapter 5)

Successful R&D projects lead to the next logical step in the new venture process (that is, full-scale production and commercial product introduction). There are numerous minor steps between R&D and commercial introduction, but we are most concerned with those requiring significant capital funds from the parent company. Most of these steps usually involve engineering tasks such as redesign for mass production, tooling design, and production layout.

Four separate, nonengineering analyses must be completed before capital funds are allocated to a full-scale commercial new venture. The analyses address markets, competitors, costs, and uncertainty (as shown in the middle portion of Figure 11-1). Market analysis is the first and usually the most important of these tasks. We have divided market analysis into two stages: (1) determination of the potential size of the market, and (2) estimation of how quickly the market will accept your new product. The potential size of the market can be estimated with the aid of (1) scenarios (written statements of possible future events), (2) needs assessments (a compilation of other people's forecasts into market potential estimates), and (3) less formal market potential approaches such as library searches and interviews with knowledgeable people.

The time required for buyers to adopt the product within your target market can be estimated with the aid of a market penetration curve. The overall shape of the curve is well documented in research on past product innovations. Innovations typically begin penetrating a new market very slowly, then accelerate for a period, and eventually slow again as market saturation is approached. Market penetration curves must be tailored to your market segment. Use of factors such as relative prices, expected profitability, and dynamic changes in competing technologies can be incorporated into a market penetration curve. Less formal means of predicting market acceptance can also be used if circumstances in your new venture do not allow the use of market penetration curves. Either means should yield forecasts of annual sales for your new venture.

When conducting the market analysis for a new venture:

DO

- Commit the resources and discipline necessary to conduct a formal market analysis.
- Begin a market analysis with an informal search of locally available data. Then regroup for a more formal analysis.
- Collect and compare other available market forecasts (from government reports, consulting firms, or economic forecasting companies).
- Include interviews with market experts, researchers, consumers, and managers who participate in current market events.
- Include price or life-cycle cost comparisons from the buyer's perspective as part of the market analysis.

DO NOT

- Assume the market will be so large that even a small percentage share will assure your success.
- Avoid a market analysis because your markets are highly uncertain or speculative.
- Assume the best market forecast is the most widely referenced forecast.
- Assume a market forecast has validity just because analytical tools were used to generate it.
- Use only one technique to conduct the market analysis.

Competition (Discussed in Chapter 6)

The reactions of competitors to the introduction of your new venture's product are important to its ability to produce economic value for the parent company. Competitive analysis is basically a set of techniques that modify the analysis of markets. One way to incorporate competitive analysis into new venture analysis is to (1) estimate the lead time of your new venture (that is, the number of years or months between the date your new venture introduces its products and the next firm introduces a competitive product), and (2) estimate the market share that you will lose once the competition has entered their product. If your new venture is introducing products into an established market, we suggest examining (1) the costs of market entry, (2) likely competitor retaliation, and (3) possible supplier and distributor problems.

The data needed to conduct a complete competitive analysis are always difficult to obtain. The techniques to analyze the data are not precise and require a great deal of judgment by the analyst. Competitive analysis is a craft that yields better results as both the analyst and the new venture management team gain experience with it.

When assessing your new venture's competition:

DO

- Use competitor analysis results to modify new venture sales forecasts.
- Clearly identify what features of your new venture are unique relative to those of competitors, and then objectively estimate how long it will take competitors to copy those features.
- Use personal contacts to collect competitor data.
- Assume that competitive pressures will grow as the market expands.
- Conduct an ongoing investigation that grows in complexity with the growth of your new venture.
- Make competitor analysis a permanent and integral element of the new venture's strategic planning process.

DO NOT

- Depend solely on cost leadership to maintain a competitive edge in your target market.
- Assume that rapid growth in your market sector will protect your venture's market share (or assure that your sales will continue to increase).

- Assume that all competitors will use the same organizational form that your venture has adopted.
- Expect to obtain a large amount of relevant data in the first attempt at a competitive assessment, or expect much quantitative analysis of that data.
- Attempt to recreate a competitor's strategic plan (unless one competitor's actions are the key determinant of your new venture's success).

Cost Analysis (Discussed in Chapter 7)

Both nonrecurring investment costs and recurring operating costs are important in estimating the economic value of a new venture. The parent company typically has extensive expertise in cost analysis. The tendency is to conduct excessive analyses on costs because they are under the direct control of the new venture. The guiding principle in new venture cost estimation should be to examine in detail only the key determinants of the product's cost.

If cost reductions over time are strategically important to the new venture, learning and experience curve techniques can be quite helpful. These curves relate costs and prices to cumulative production of the product. The validity and usefulness of the curves have been questioned because they do not explicitly indicate why the cost reductions are expected. The analyst should clearly specify what factor or factors will cause the cost reductions before estimating learning curve slopes. The most appropriate way to use learning curves is to relate them to individual components of your product. These component learning curves can then be summed to see the impact on your product's total cost.

When evaluating the costs of your new venture's products:

DO

- Take a broad view of new venture costs including taxes, insurance, and other costs usually considered only at the corporate headquarters level.
- Consider only the incremental cost impacts of the new venture on the parent company.
- Estimate nonrecurring development and capital costs beginning at the lowest level of equipment aggregation possible.
- Explicitly incorporate cost dynamics if they play a role in the new venture's strategy.

- Formulate and use standard definitions of learning curves and experience curves.

- Estimate learning curve slopes for individual components of your product and then sum them to estimate the entire product's cost trend.

- Clearly understand what cost factors are causing the cost reductions predicted by the learning curve analysis.

DO NOT

- Spend excessive amounts of time or resources in the analysis of costs at the expense of market and competitor analyses.

- Depend on rules of thumb in estimating capital or production costs.

- Assume costs will continue to decline even if demand rises very rapidly (that is, if a seller's market arises).

- Underestimate the past experience that is applicable to the learning curves used in your new venture.

- Design a cost accounting system as part of a new venture cost analysis.

Uncertainty Assessment (Discussed in Chapter 8)

Uncertainty is the hallmark of new ventures. The successful assessment of new ventures requires that uncertainty be understood to the maximum extent possible. The objective of uncertainty analysis is to balance your new venture risks with its expected returns. The goal is not to choose the new venture with the least risk. Uncertainty can be handled by (1) sensitivity analyses (which separately varies each new venture parameter and investigates its impact on the economic value of the venture), (2) scenario analysis (which varies groups of key parameters at the same time), (3) decision tree analysis (which incorporates the probabilities of various new venture outcomes into the analysis), (4) Monte Carlo or other simulations (which further refine the probabilities of various outcomes), and (5) techniques that encode managers' attitudes toward risk and then incorporate those attitudes into the uncertainty analysis.

When assessing the uncertainty of a new venture:

DO

- Consider new venture risks separately from risks taken in the parent company's established product lines.

- Keep the uncertainty of the new venture in the perspective of its expected returns.
- Determine how uncertainty will be estimated before building an integrating analysis framework for the new venture.
- Begin estimation of uncertainty with a sensitivity analysis on all assumptions.
- Predict, as an intuitive check on the results, the impact of each sensitivity on the summary measure of economic value before running the integrating model.
- Keep the sensitivity analysis well organized and documented.
- Explore who pays the consequential damages if an insured event occurs and include that analysis as part of the uncertainty assessment.
- Investigate factors that will probably move in compensating directions over time and thereby mitigate some risks of the new venture.
- Clearly state which intangible benefits and costs are excluded from the uncertainty analysis.

DO NOT

- Fill your company's new venture portfolio with only low-risk ventures.
- Depend on insurance to cover any crucial risks of a new venture.
- Limit the uncertainty analysis to only explicit assumptions used in the integrating model of the new venture.
- Forget that key people within the new venture can leave.
- Attempt to explicitly incorporate risk attitudes into the uncertainty analysis without the prior support of senior management.

Integration and Decision Making (Discussed in Chapter 9)

The separate analyses addressing markets, costs, competitors, and uncertainty need to be integrated in order to get an overall picture of the economic value of your new venture. We have found that the best way to accomplish this integration is by constructing a computer-based model of the new venture. The model should simulate the year-to-year behavior of your target market and all its participants. It should be designed to produce yearly balance sheets, income statements, and funds flow statements. Those results should then be summarized using a measure of the new venture's economic value such as internal rate of return or net present value.

The results of the integrating model and the other new venture analyses should be presented in a brief but concise business plan. The business plan should evolve into the new venture's strategic plan as the venture matures. The results of the new venture analysis probably will be presented in numerous management meetings. The analyst's responsibility includes the clear and concise communication of the results of the new venture analysis. The amount of time and resources spent preparing those presentations should be commensurate with their importance.

When integrating and presenting a new venture analysis:

DO

- Design the integrating model to reflect the unique circumstances of your new venture including the dynamic interactions between buyers, competitors, and your venture.

- Allow the integrating model to evolve in complexity and subtlety over time.

- Use the integrating model to conduct the uncertainty analysis.

- Use internal rate of return and net present value as the summary measures of the new venture's economic value.

- Use the expected cash flows of the venture as the basis for the economic value calculation.

- Design the integrating model to produce annual pro forma income statements, balance sheets, and funds flow statements.

- Prepare a concise 30- to 50-page business plan and periodically update it.

DO NOT

- Begin improvements or restructuring of the integrating model before a simple version is operational and sensitivities have been analyzed.

- Rely on payback or return on investment (ROI) as the summary measures of economic attractiveness.

- Include expected interest costs as an expense in the internal rate of return and net present value calculations.

- Forget that competitors will retaliate as your sales begin to grow.

- Forget to explicitly model key constraints or delays that your new venture may face (for example, capacity constraints, hiring constraints, or regulatory/legal constraints).

- Forget tax impacts and special tax credits or other tax subsidies available to your new venture.
- Forget to model the continuing impacts of your venture's R&D program.
- Add complexities to the model that the input data cannot support or that are not understandable by management.
- Underestimate the importance of presentations to the usefulness of the new venture analysis results.

New Venture Portfolios and New Venture Finance (Discussed in Chapter 10)

Careful selection of the projects that comprise your company's new venture portfolio can yield a more balanced approach that has more certainty of being successful. The analysis of a new venture portfolio should expose the trade-offs between important but opposing factors that will influence the outcomes of new ventures. The analysis can begin by developing simple graphs showing the trade-offs between pairs of key factors (for example, expected returns versus risks, or target market segments versus stage of new venture development). Further refinement and complexity can be added to the analysis as insights into the nature of the firm's new venture portfolio are gained.

Questions will continually arise regarding how new ventures within an existing firm should be financed. We strongly recommend that new ventures be considered as internal investments of your company that tap the same general sources of funds (that is, retained earnings and company issued debt and equity) as more traditional investments. Special external financing sources should only be sought as a last resort. If such sources are used, the parent company should be prepared to give up a significant amount of the new venture's expected profits, management control, or both. The objective of the parent company should be clearly specified before external financing is sought.

When reviewing your company's new venture portfolio:

DO

- Examine risk and return trade-offs between new ventures currently being pursued.
- Examine the market, technology, and customer diversity of your new venture portfolio to better predict how the combined economic value of your new ventures will be affected by changing future events.

- Begin your portfolio review with simple trade-off charts and move to more complex analyses later.
- Experiment with alternative ways to examine trade-offs and develop an approach that fits your firm's situation.
- Establish a mechanism to allow any intrapreneur to reenter the mainstream of the business if his new venture is terminated.

DO NOT

- Depend on a single technology, market, or customer for the success of most new ventures in your portfolio.
- Allow most of your firm's new ventures to be in the same stage of development.
- Include only low-risk new ventures in your portfolio.
- Use analytical approaches to portfolio assessment that require quantifiable measures of risk.

When financing your new venture portfolio:

DO

- Clarify the parent company's objective for the new venture before seeking external financing.
- Shop around for financial advisers and investors whose objectives are well matched to your new venture's goals.
- Understand the total costs of the external financing vehicle before it is implemented.

DO NOT

- Address financing issues until the decision to pursue the new venture has been approved.
- Pursue external financing until all internal financing avenues are closed.
- Vary the level of internal financing support to new ventures to meet short-term financial goals of the parent corporation.
- Underestimate the value of the tax, legal, and financial expertise housed within the parent company when preparing for external new venture financing.

Selected Additional References

Abell, D. F. "Strategic Windows." *Journal of Marketing,* July 1978, pp. 21–26.

Abell, D. F., and J. S. Hammond. *Strategic Market Planning.* Englewood Cliffs, N.J.: Prentice-Hall, 1979.

Abernathy and Kline, "Managing Our Way to Economic Decline." *Harvard Business Review,* July, August 1980, pp. 67–77.

Asher, H. "Cost Quantity Relationships in the Airframe Industry." Santa Monica, Calif.: The Rand Corporation, 1956.

Ayres, R. U. *Technological Forecasting and Long-Range Planning.* New York: McGraw-Hill, 1969.

Baker, N. R. "R&D Project Selection Models: An Assessment." *IEEE Transactions on Engineering Management* EM-21, no. 4 (November 1974).

Baker, N. R., and J. R. Freeland. "Recent Advances in R&D Value Measurement." Invited Paper, 41st National Meeting of the Operations Research Society of America (ORSA), New Orleans, Louisiana, April 1972.

BDM Corporation, *Photovoltaic Power Systems Market Identification and Analysis* Vol. 3. McLean, Va.: BDM Corporation, 1978.

Beattie, D. W. "Marketing a New Product." *Operations Research Quarterly* 20 (December 1969), pp. 429–35.

Blackman, A. W., Jr. "The Rate of Innovation in the Commercial Aircraft Jet Engine Market." *Technological Forecasting and Social Change* 2 (May 1971).

————. "A Mathematical Model for Trend Forecasts." *Technological Forecasting and Social Change* 3 (June 1972).

————. "New Venture Planning: The Role of Technological Forecasting." *Technological Forecasting and Social Change* 5 (September 1973), pp. 25–49.

————. "The Market Dynamics of Technological Substitution." *Technological Forecasting and Social Change* 6 (October 1974).

Bodde, D. L. "Riding the Experience Curve." *Technology Review,* March, April 1976.

Boston Consulting Group, Inc. *Perspectives on Experience.* Boston, Mass.: Boston Consulting Group, 1968.

Bright, J. R. and M. E. F. Schoeman, eds. *A Guide to Practical Technological Forecasting.* Englewood Cliffs, N.J.: Prentice-Hall, 1973.

Brown, R. V.; A. S. Kahr; and C. Peterson. *Decision Analysis: An Overview.* New York: Holt, Rinehart & Winston, 1974.

Calder, B. J. "Focus Groups and the Nature of Qualitative Marketing Research." *Journal of Marketing Research* 14 (August 1977), pp. 353–64.

Candea, Hax A., and Karmarker. "Economic and Social Evaluation of Capital Investment Decisions—An Application." In *Studies in Operations Management,* ed. A. C. Hax. North Holland Press, 1978.

Cetron, M. J. *Technological Forecasting, A Practical Approach.* New York: Technology Forecasting Institute, 1969.

Cetron, M. J. and D. N. Overly. "Disagreeing with the Future." *Technology Review,* March, April 1973, pp. 10–16.

Christensen, C.; K. R. Andrews; and J. L. Bower. *Business Policy, Text and Cases.* Homewood, Ill.: Richard D. Irwin, 1978.

Chrystie, T. L. and F. J. Fabozzi, eds. *Left Hand Financing: An Emerging Field of Corporate Finance.* Homewood, Ill.: Dow Jones-Irwin, 1983.

Clark, C. and L. Schkade. *Statistical Methods for Business Decisions.* Dallas, Tex.: South-Western Publishing, 1969.

Clark, J. J.; T. J. Hindelang; and R. E. Pritchard. *Capital Budgeting, Planning and Control of Capital Expenditures.* Englewood Cliffs, N.J.: Prentice-Hall, 1979.

Conrad, G. R., and I. H. Plotkin. "Risk/Return: U.S. Industry Pattern." *Harvard Business Review,* March, April 1968, pp. 90–99.

Cooper, M. J. "An Evaluation System for Project Selection." *Research Management* 21 (July 1978), pp. 29–33.

Costello, D. and D. Posner. "An Overview of Photovoltaic Market Research." *Solar Cells* 1 (January 1979), pp. 37–53.

Costello, D.; D. Posner; D. Schiffel; J. Doane; and C. Bishop. *Photovoltaic*

Venture Analysis, Final Report. 3 vols. SERI/TR-52-040, Solar Energy Research Institute. Washington, D.C.: U.S. Department of Energy, 1978.

Cox, K. K.; J. B. Higginbotham; and J. Burton. "Application of Focus Group Interviews in Marketing." *Journal of Marketing* 40 (January 1976), pp. 77–80.

Dalby, J. "Practical Refinements to the Cross-Impact Matrix Technique of Technological Forecasting." In *Industrial Applications of Technological Forecasting: Its Utilization in R&D Management,* eds. J. Cetron and C. A. Ralph. New York: John Wiley & Sons, 1971.

E. I. du Pont de Nemours and Company, Inc. *Du Pont Guide to Venture Analysis (A Framework for Venture Planning).* Wilmington, Del.: E. I. du Pont de Nemours and Co., 1971, p. 42.

Energy Resources Inc. *Case Study Applications of Venture Analysis: Fluidized Bed.* Prepared for U.S. Department of Energy (Contract no. EX-77-C-01-2687), Cambridge, Mass.: Energy Resources Company, Inc., April 1979.

Financial Executives Research Foundation. *Mergers and Acquisitions: Planning and Actions.* New York: Financial Executives Research Foundation, 1963.

Fisher, J. C., and R. H. Pry. "A Simple Substitution Model of Technological Change." *Technological Forecasting and Social Change* 3 (June 1971).

Fruham, W. *Financial Strategy: Studies in the Creation, Transfer and Destruction of Shareholder Value.* Homewood, Ill.: Richard D. Irwin, 1979.

Glazebrook, K. D. "Some Ranking Formulae for Alternative Research Projects." *Omega* 6 no. 2 (February 1978), pp. 193–4.

Hamilton, H. R. "Screening Business Development Opportunities." *Business Horizons,* August 1974, pp. 13–24.

Hax, A. C., and N. S. Majluf. "A Methodological Approach For the Development of Strategic Planning in Diversified Corporations." In *Studies in Operations Management,* ed. A. Hax. New York: Elsevier-North Holland Publishing, 1978, pp. 41–98.

Hax, A. C., and K. M. Wiig. "The Use of Decision Analysis in Capital Investment Problems." *Sloan Management Review,* 1976, pp. 19–48.

Hirsch, W. B. "Manufacturing Progress Functions." *Review of Economics and Statistics* 34 (May 1952).

Hirschmann, W. B. "Profit From the Learning Curve." *Harvard Business Review* 42, no. 1 (January, February 1964), pp. 125–39.

Hollander, S. *The Sources of Increased Efficiency, A Study of Du Pont Rayon Plants.* Cambridge, Mass.: MIT Press, 1965.

Howard, R. A. "Decision Analysis: Applied Decision Theory." In *Proceedings of the Fourth International Conference on Operational Research,* eds. D. B. Hertz, and J. Mekre. New York: John Wiley & Sons, 1968.

Hudson, R. G. et al. "New Product Planning Decision Under Uncertainty." *Interfaces* 8 pt. 2 (November 1977), pp. 82–96.

Jones, H. and B. Twiss. *Forecasting Technology for Planning Decisions.* New York: MacMillan, 1978, pp. 141–53.

Kabas, I. "You Can Bank on Uncertainty." *Harvard Business Review,* May, June 1976, pp. 95–105.

Karger, D. W., and R. Murdick. *New Product Venture Management.* New York: Gordon and Breach, 1972.

Lenz, R. C. Jr., and H. W. Lanford. "The Substitution Phenomenon." *Business Horizons,* February 1972.

Linstone, H. A., and M. Turoff, eds. *The Delphi Method: Techniques and Applications.* Reading, Mass.: Addison-Wesley Publishing, 1975.

Lipstein, B. "Critique of: "A New Product Analysis and Decision Model." *Management Science* 14, no. 8 (April 1968), pp. B-518-19.

Mansfield, E. "Technical Change and the Rate of Imitation." *Econometrica* 29, no. 4 (October 1961).

Marguis, D. G. "The Anatomy of Successful Innovation." *Innovation* 1, no. 7 (1969), pp. 28–37.

Mason, R. H., and Goudzwaard. "Performance of Conglomerate Firms: A Portfolio Approach." *Journal of Finance* 31 (March 1976), pp. 39–49.

Merriam, D. W. and J. W. Wilkinson. "Model for Planning and Feedforward Control." *Managerial Planning,* March, April 1977, pp. 31–40.

Miller, E. M. "Uncertainty Induced Bias in Capital Budgeting." *Financial Management* 7 (Autumn 1978), pp. 12–18.

Moscato, D. R. *Building Financial Decision Making Models: An Introduction to Principles and Procedures.* New York: American Management Associations, 1980.

Naylor, H. *Corporate Planning Models.* Reading, Mass.: Addison-Wesley Publishing, 1979.

Pessemier, E. A. *Product Management: Strategy and Organization.* New York: John Wiley & Sons, 1977.

Peterson, R. W. "New Venture Management in a Large Company." *Harvard Business Review,* May, June 1967, p. 68.

Porter, M. E. *Competitive Strategy: Techniques for Analyzing Industry and Competitors.* New York: Free Press, 1980, pp. 344–45.

Rivett, P. *Principles of Model Building.* New York: John Wiley & Sons, 1972.

Roberts, E. B. "Exploratory and Normative Technical Forecasting: A Critical Appraisal." *Technological Forecasting* 1 (March 1969), pp. 113–27.

————. "New Ventures for Corporate Growth." *Harvard Business Review*, July, August 1980, pp. 134–42.

Rumelt, R. *Strategy, Structure and Implementation*. Cambridge, Mass.: Harvard Univ. Press, 1974.

Rummel, R. J. *Applied Factor Analysis*. Evanston, Ill.: Northwestern University Press, 1970.

Sackman, H. *Delphi Critique: Expert Opinion, Forecasting and Group Process*. Lexington, Mass.: Lexington Books, 1975.

Salter, M. S., and W. A. Weinhold. *Diversification Through Acquisition*. New York: Free Press, 1979.

Samuelson, P. *Economics*. New York: McGraw-Hill, 1980.

Schiffel, D.; D. Costello; D. Posner; and D. Witholder. *The Market Penetration of Solar Energy: A Model Review Workshop Summary*. Golden, Colo.: Solar Energy Research Institute, SERI-16, 1978.

Sharpe, W. F. *Portfolio Theory and Capital Market*. New York: McGraw-Hill, 1970.

Simon, H. A. *The New Science of Management Decision*. New York: Harper & Row, 1960.

Slocum, D. H. *New Venture Methodology*. New York: American Management Association, 1972.

Souder, W. E. "A Scoring Methodology for Assessing the Suitability of Management Science Models." *Management Science* 18, no. 10. (June 1972), pp. B-526–43.

Spetzler, C. S. "The Development of a Corporate Risk Policy for Capital Investment Decisions." *Readings in Decision Analysis*. (Decision Analysis Group), Palo Alto, Calif.: SRI International, Inc.,1977, pp. 469-90.

Spetzler, C. S., and R. Zamora. "Decision Analysis of a Facilities Investment and Expansion Problem." *Readings in Decision Analysis* Decision Analysis Group. Palo Alto, Calif.: SRI International, Inc. 1977, pp. 203–33.

Stern, M. O. et al. "A Model for Forecasting the Substitution of One Technology for Another." *Technological Forecasting and Social Change* 7 (November 1975).

Thermo Electron Corporation. *Venture Analysis Case Study: Steam Rankine Recovery Cycle Producing Electric Power from Waste Heat*. Cambridge, Mass.: Thermo Electron Inc., December 1978.

Tryon, R. C., and D. E. Bailey. *Cluster Analysis*. New York: McGraw-Hill, 1970.

Urban, G. L. "A New Product Analysis and Decision Model." *Management Science* 14, no. 8 (April 1968), pp. B-490–17.

Urban, G. L., and J. Hauser. *Design and Marketing of New Products*. Englewood Cliffs, N.J.: Prentice-Hall, 1980.

Weston, F. S., and E. F. Brigham. *Essentials of Managerial Finance.* 7th ed. Hinsdale, Ill.: Dryden Press, 1981.

William, D. J. "A Study of a Decision Model for R&D Project Selection." *Operational Research Quarterly* 20, no. 3 (1969), pp. 361–73.

Wolf, M., and J. Greenberg. "Solar Photovoltaic Systems and Learning Curves." *Astronautics and Aeronautics,* February 1976.

Young, G. R., and B. Standish, Jr. *Joint Ventures: Planning and Action.* New York: Financial Executive Research Foundation, 1977.

Index